Chelsea,
Stay healthy +
Enjoy the Book!
Love your office
Cathy

HEALTH
WELL
DONE

HEALTH

CATHY DOLAN-SCHWEITZER

HEALTH
WELL
DONE

A People-Centered
Management Approach to
Building Healthcare
Environments

First Printing: 2018

ISBN: 978-0-9992509-0-7

Health Well Done

92 Main Street

Yonkers, NY 10701

Website: www.healthwelldone.com

E-mail: Cathy@healthwelldone.com

Special discounts are available on quantity purchases by corporations, associations, educators, and others. Contact the publisher for additional details.

Cover design by Miladinka Milic

Interior design by Avenue A Design Studio

I would like to dedicate this book
to my dad, whose life principles
and sense of humor shaped my life
and influenced who I am today.

Dad, I know that you are watching
over me with a big smile.

TABLE OF CONTENTS

FOREWORD

At the very foundation of our work in creating optimal healthcare environments lies the understanding that the built environment can contribute to better outcomes for patients and safer work environments for staff, as well as support friends and family members in their roles as active members of the care process.

One of the many strategies that we employ to achieve these goals is to design and build spaces that promote collaboration among staff, caregivers, patients, and family members, and that facilitate better health outcomes by encouraging communication and engagement. It's difficult to get to this end point without having a collaborative and diverse team of knowledgeable experts and stakeholders in place from the start. Yet assembling a multidisciplinary team is just the beginning. Knowing how to foster a healthy culture within the team, and how to organize and maximize the efforts of individual members, requires a carefully considered plan and a strong project management process, both vital to the success of any healthcare project.

It's no easy job to manage all the parts and personalities of a project, no matter its size, and in healthcare there's the added responsibility of addressing life safety issues. That's why distilling a plan down to a simple project management process that follows the three-step integrated approach of *Healthy Patient, Healthy Team,* and *Healthy Project* is a roadmap to success.

I first got to know Cathy Dolan-Schweitzer when she joined The Center for Health Design's all-volunteer Environmental Standards

Council (ESC). The ESC is a multidisciplinary group that engages in standards-related initiatives and advocacy, successfully working with such groups as The Joint Commission and the Facilities Guidelines Institute. Cathy is known to many for her impressive ability to corral groups of passionate, strong-minded individuals. This asset and her decades of healthcare and project management experience inform every page of *Health Well Done*, making it an invaluable resource for project managers, leaders, and stakeholders looking to build healthy environments for their patients and who have a deep desire to get it right.

Health Well Done will change how you design and build patient-centered healthcare environments by helping you expand your project focus to include an understanding of healing. It will also provide you with the practical hands-on tools that you will need to build a strong foundation upon which to base the right balance of processes to achieve your goals. The end result: healthcare environments that put patients first.

Debra Levin, EDAC

President and Chief Executive Officer
The Center for Health Design
www.HealthDesign.org

THE VALUE OF A HEALTHCARE PROJECT WELL DONE

"Healthy citizens are the greatest asset any country can have."

— Winston Churchill

In the years since the enactment of the Affordable Care Act, expanded access to healthcare has spurred a concurrent rise in the construction of new outpatient facilities and repurposing of existing hospital spaces and infrastructure. This ongoing evolution of healthcare systems and services is in turn driving considerable rethinking of how clinical space planning can yield greater benefits to patients—including quality outcomes—and improve institutional revenue streams. Clearly, for any individual or organization entrusted with creating or transforming healthcare facility space, this is the time to "get it right."

Part of getting things right, however, is being able to navigate through shifting political winds and a patient-centered healthcare economy. This means accommodating today's savvy healthcare consumers, who are better educated, expect more for their care, and can seek out transparent, competitive healthcare options on the Internet. It is for these and other reasons that managers who are assigned to facilitate the creation of patient-centered healthcare environments (PCEs) must ensure that healthcare systems are able to connect with patients and their families—the end users—and meet their needs.

However, building a PCE is a complex process that relies on the contributions of dozens of professionals from many different fields, as well as on buy-in from patients, families, institutional staff, and the broader community. Significant practical challenges come with undertaking such projects, from concerns involving population health, regulatory standards, hospital productivity, financial challenges, and LEED (Leadership in Energy and Environmental Design) certification to arriving at designs that are truly patient-centric and contribute to the overall productivity and well-being of staff. Planners, designers, and builders—and those of us who lead these individuals through project teams—should all recognize that the way in which projects are approached will have a profound impact on the delivery of optimal patient care and contribute overall to the collective health of Americans. This is the driving principle behind *Health Well Done*.

How You Manage a Project Matters

Visiting a healthcare facility is often a highly stressful time for patients, many of whom might arrive at their appointments filled with fear, worry, and uncertainty. Will their surroundings reassure them and ease any negative feelings or will their anxieties be heightened by what they encounter? And what about staff members who face occupational stresses day in and day out in the same surroundings?

Stress is insidiously damaging. According to Dr. Herbert Benson, a Harvard professor and the founder of the Mind/Body Medical Institute at Massachusetts General Hospital, toxic thinking literally "wears down" the brain and the rest of the body and can lead to stress, which affects our body's natural healing capacity. The negative effects can be profound and extensive. According to the institute's website, "roughly 60 to 90 percent of doctor visits are for conditions related to stress."[1]

It is unsurprising, therefore, that calm, stress-free healthcare environments can have tangible, measurable benefits. In fact, research suggests a strong link between the design of healthcare settings and outcomes experienced by patients and staff. In preparing their 2004 report to The Center for Health Design, Roger Ulrich and colleagues sifted through thousands of scientific articles and found more than 600 studies—most in top peer-reviewed journals—on the impact of hospital design on staff and quality outcomes. They developed scorecards to assess the strength of evidence presented in each paper on the link between aspects of the healthcare environment and clinical outcomes, including healthcare quality, patient safety, and patient and staff stress. Their meta-analysis found substantial support for the important role that environmental settings play in improved patient safety and healing (including fewer medical errors and infection rates) and in reduced stress in patients and staff.[2]

With evidenced-based information in hand, it would seem logical to have research inform our every decision regarding the design of healing (stress-reducing) environments. After all, who would argue against making patients feel relaxed, safe, well treated, and in capable hands? Unfortunately, it takes time, sometimes years, for research projects to yield conclusions. Given the fast pace of institutional developments in the healthcare industry, data that could potentially guide efforts might not be available. So as the wait for additional research continues, you as a project manager should continue investigating novel ideas for designing and building a PCE.

As you do so, here are important points to remember:

1   Idea development takes money and other resources, but the "magic" only happens by applying the project team's collective wisdom and experience to project tasks.

2   Innovation and the successful implementation of new ideas come out of an environment of learning.

3   A willingness to accept failure is required when developing the right idea for an environment that will best serve the patient. In a Geekwire.com interview, technology entrepreneur Jeff Bezos explained that, "If you want to be inventive, you have to experiment a lot, which means you will fail a lot."[3]

The Nature of the Beast

It is important to recognize from the outset that healthcare is not a product manufactured by a system. According to Dr. Maren

Batalden, Associate Chief Quality Officer at Cambridge Health Alliance in Massachusetts, administering healthcare is a "process of co-production," where "health outcomes are not created by healthcare professionals acting alone. They're always co-created with patients."[4] With this in mind, and in the face of a competitive field and a cost-containment culture, healthcare systems are trying to up their game. Finding innovative, successful ways to help patients become well and stay well is more urgent than ever.

One answer is to build a cost-effective, sustainable healthcare environment that supports the delivery of the best possible patient-centered care by addressing the needs and perspectives of patients, their families, and the institution's staff. A properly designed and built PCE offers a safe, comfortable, and calming backdrop for healing to take place by allowing staff to do their jobs properly and, more important, by helping patients concentrate on transitioning from illness to wellness. Patients know when they are put first, and the depth of their gratitude can run deep, as seen in people who recover from illness to later embark on careers in healthcare, or when former patients become angels of financial support for an institution.

No Longer Business As Usual

In your past management of the design, building, and implementation of healthcare environments, did you achieve your goals by focusing mainly on budget, schedules, and build specifications? Or did you consider the circumstances and perspectives of the end users? And how did the decisions made by you and your team ultimately manifest in the final environment?

If you have unintentionally focused solely on the bottom line to the exclusion of other considerations, you are not alone. I myself have fallen into this trap. I was taught to get the job done and think in concrete, logical ways, prioritizing for budgets and schedules and sacrificing all else to get the project done. *Health Well Done* takes an entirely different tack, asking the question: Can my project be done or can it be well done?

"Well done" means kicking off a project with a project team that genuinely cares about how patients will feel in the environment and how they will be able to connect mindfully, spiritually, or aesthetically with it. Well done means that the team understands how patient care outcomes can be affected by the way in which patients and staff interact and use a space. Well done also means that a team is willing to work in a collaborative spirit, where the definition of success extends beyond the physical construction of a space. In other words, the team is committed to providing patients with the opportunity to heal and feel great, as well as to supporting staff productivity and commitment to patient care by letting their collective wisdom and experience inform innovations in operations and workflows.

Prioritizing for patients and staff also has the very important benefit of enhancing a healthcare system's reputation—which is critical given the value of an institution's brand, personality, and patient care philosophy—and of reinforcing its commitment to staff.

At the heart of it all, well done means that a team will come away from a finished PCE project thinking, "Wow! We really accomplished something significant together!"

The Genesis of Health Well Done

Transformative change in a physical environment cannot come without transformative change in how that environment comes into being. I learned this lesson in a deeply personal way. Prior to my developing the *Health Well Done* approach, I had been successfully leading teams of design and construction professionals in their efforts to build high-quality PCEs. We measured our "success" by positive feedback elicited from patients, the medical professionals who treated them, and other employees of the healthcare system. We distributed Press Ganey surveys to patients and received consistently high patient-satisfaction scores through Hospital Consumer Assessment of Healthcare Providers and Systems (HCAPS) surveys. Hence, I remained satisfied with my work for many years, until 2011, when I unexpectedly found myself sitting opposite my doctor, who told me that I would need to undergo six months of cancer treatment. It was during this difficult time as a patient that I fully experienced the tangible results of the decisions made by people like me who built hospital environments.

Throughout my treatment and recovery, I spent a great deal of time thinking about my past work with project teams and ultimately realized that my north star had always been the bottom line. Budgets and schedules drove many decisions, and while many professionals might not think that this is a bad thing, is it the best thing?

Once an approved project commences, it does not always proceed efficiently, since people and companies with different agendas often jockey for position. There might not be a clearly established scope, especially regarding resources. Worse yet, the schedule might be driving the project: "Your deadline is X. Do whatever it takes to meet it." The knee-jerk response is often, "Yes, absolutely!" As the project manager, the last thing you want is to be handed a half-baked project by your boss with the expectation to just get it done.

This is a common problem in healthcare because of the speed at which providers are trying to adapt a new idea, service line, or technology-driven initiative to their existing system. When you are assigned a project in a chaotic manner, the situation immediately becomes stress-inducing. Everything feels scattered, rushed, moving in all directions, and you might feel your cortisol levels rise from the pressure of adhering to an impossible schedule. The fallout can have a serious impact on your management of the project. You might find yourself with shorter timelines for construction drawings and contractor pricing, forced to opt for quick-ship furniture, or unable to invite the right people to join your team. I always say that if you do not spend enough time up front properly planning a project, you will pay for it in the end with change orders and other costs and delays.

These are just a few of the potential negative consequences of applying a typical process-centric approach to building a PCE. Instead, what if institutional and community healthcare projects were managed using a people-centric approach? As project leader, you would first establish the intention to build a people-centered environment and do so by gathering facts and piecing together a detailed picture of the project's vision and scope. You would slow down to view the project as representing more than just a physical structure or space.

Sy Syms, the founder of a well-known clothing chain, coined the phrase, "An educated consumer is our best customer."

This nugget of wisdom applies here. A people-centric approach to building healthcare environments involves answering the needs of educated patients and caring about how all stakeholders will be affected.

Healthy Patient, Healthy Team, Healthy Project

The *Health Well Done* project management system is built on three thematic principles that are followed to create an effective, empowering, and supportive PCE: *Healthy Patient, Healthy Team,* and *Healthy Project.* By understanding the importance of each of these areas of focus and considering their requirements, you and your team will be able to optimally design, plan, and navigate to completion a PCE project that is not merely done, but well done. So, what exactly do these three components stand for?

Healthy Patient asks the question, "Who is the patient?" Because at the end of the day, this is why everyone is at the table and why you have a project budget and schedule in the first place. The concept of *Healthy Patient* describes all of us in both wellness and illness and is based on whatever disease we are fighting at the time and on how we can become our best selves as we move along the care continuum to wellness. This requires us to actively participate in our care by, among other actions, educating ourselves, actively monitoring our vitals, exercising more, reducing our caloric intake, and working in partnership with clinicians to arrive at the best course of care.

This rethink of the patient-provider relationship is increasingly important, since hospitals today are no longer the "fixers" but the "preventers" and should serve as places where, ideally, people can learn about caring for the mind, body, and spirit. In addition, the fact that we are living longer is forcing us to think about our finances when thinking about our health. For example, if you want to work well beyond the traditional retirement age, you really have no choice but to be healthy. As a result, patients today are demanding more from healthcare. They want to feel secure in their choices of providers and healthcare environments. How a project team envisions and builds such an environment will make all the difference when it comes to patient trust and loyalty.

Healthy Team describes a group of participants who work under a "common intention" and collaborate effectively to complete a PCE project. At the center of a *Healthy Team* is the project leader, who must ably orchestrate the activities of a diverse internal and external collective of stakeholders—from clinicians, nurses, administrators, and engineers to finance, IT, construction, and building services personnel, and others. It is through open communication, strong connections and relationships, ongoing support at every phase, and proactive, creative problem solving with these professionals that good project leaders become great at leveraging their team's talents and experiences.

Healthy Project relies on a *Healthy Team* and an articulated goal. It forms the backbone of your efforts and is a way to document all the information that you have collected from working with your *Healthy Team,* with whom you have established stability through communication, organization, and goal setting. *Healthy Project* provides the reliable methodologies for shepherding the project from start to finish. It involves the nuts and bolts of the project, including the budget, the scope of work, the formal project management process (for example, construction schedules and disruptions to normal operations), the healing component, sustainability, and LEED certification. *Healthy Project* relies on evidence-based design (meaning that design elements chosen have been shown to improve care, boost morale, and save money), integrates Eastern and Western healing modalities, goes green when possible, and generates a high return on involvement and investment.

What You Will Learn

The first three chapters of this book delve in more detail on the foundational components of a *Health Well Done* approach to healthcare project management and cover the critical aspects of getting a project done right, including understanding the project's mission, getting to know the team, establishing goals, executing key steps, avoiding pitfalls during the design and build phases, closing out a project, and making the most of lessons learned. Each chapter provides an overview followed by a practical "nuts and bolts" section filled with ideas, tips, and to-dos for navigating your way through a project's life cycle.

Chapter 4 is devoted to the art of storytelling because it is a profoundly important tool used to support every aspect of *Health Well Done*—from assembling teams to managing projects to their completion. Storytelling is a vehicle for communicating and getting things right. This chapter also features a nuts and bolts section.

Since managing a project is not always about doing something right, but also about dealing with unexpected roadblocks and minor disasters, Chapter 5 presents real-world scenarios that illustrate how projects can be sidelined or compromised, along with advice on how to avoid common issues.

Chapter 6 examines future trends and challenges in healthcare and how the *Health Well Done* project management approach can help you navigate uncharted waters. It also discusses the importance of personal responsibility for a project (and the reward that comes from helping others), and the influence of our collective health on the global community.

Finally, a resources section filled with references and links to templates, checklists, and other practical project management aids, will help you stay organized and on task.

Conclusion

It is my goal that *Health Well Done* will become your go-to guide for handling the key aspects of building a PCE project from start to finish. By being better able to collect valuable input from team members and other stakeholders, leverage talent and experience, and identify and resolve issues concerning the people and process behind your project, you will not only become a more effective leader and project manager, but you will also succeed in creating an environment that is truly patient centered. As you work your way through this book, I invite you to also visit www.HealthWellDone.com to continue your learning journey.

1

HEALTHY PATIENT

"The greatest wealth is health."

— Virgil

Healthy Patient is a reminder that all the budgeting, planning, and building of a patient-centered healthcare environment (PCE) ultimately revolve around the key end user: the patient. As a construct, *Healthy Patient* supports the relationship between the patient and the healthcare provider. It represents the importance of treating not only the body, but also the mind and spirit. It also considers the patient's family and recognizes that human interaction, kindness, and compassion are integral to the healing process.

As I mentioned in the Introduction, a *Healthy Patient* is each and all of us and is based on whatever healthcare concern we are addressing at the time and on how we can be our best selves at any point on the continuum of illness to wellness. A *Healthy Patient* is an informed participant in care who takes the initiative to self-educate and track his or her health status. More broadly, it refers to an active partnership between patients and their clinicians to establish and achieve goals for optimal healthcare.

Self-advocacy and strong patient-provider relationships are critical requisites for ensuring the delivery of the right kind of care, given the growing trend for healthcare systems to also be places to which patients can go to learn to care for themselves holistically. Of course, preventive care is a vital concern in helping us live longer and with a better quality of life. Yet although greater longevity is a good thing, how will we manage to keep ourselves healthy in the United States, where healthcare options are ever-changing and ever more expensive? *Healthy Patient* recognizes this foremost worry that individuals carry for themselves and for their loved ones, which is the basis upon which a dedicated healthcare system must develop its mission.

Catering to the Healthcare Consumer

Gone are the days when patients might take the news of a life-changing illness lying down. Never before have patients been so educated about their health and healthcare costs or so invested in choosing health insurance. As employees seek better benefits, employers are finding ways to reduce the cost of the business of health. Unfortunately, costs continue to rise as do coverage restrictions.

When it comes to healthcare options, many people are not fully informed or know what criteria to apply when judging the value of services. Cost uncertainty makes seeking healthcare more stressful than it already is or should be. However, given that the quality of healthcare can profoundly affect us at work and at home, we have no choice but to be educated customers. The need for vigilance is not just a personal one. As Americans, we must recognize that individual health has a collective impact on the nation as a whole. The Integrated Benefits Institute (IBI), which represents major U.S. employers and business coalitions, states that poor health costs the U.S. economy $576 billion annually. Of this amount, 39 percent, or $227 billion, represents lost productivity from employee absenteeism due to illness, or from what researchers call "presenteeism" (when employees report to work but illness keeps them from performing at their best).[1]

There is a reason that everyone in the United States is worried about the economy and healthcare," noted Thomas Parry, IBI's president emeritus, when speaking on the 2012 presidential election. "These are two fundamental issues that are tightly coupled through health's impact on productivity and shape our standards of living. Illness costs this country hundreds of billions of dollars, and this should serve as a wake-up call for both candidates and employers to invest in the health of workers, for the sake of the people and the benefit of U.S. business."[2]

Businesses know that profitability is tied to employee productivity and that healthy, happy, and satisfied employees are more likely to be productive. Many companies no longer offer employees a health insurance plan and leave it at that. This is because company attitudes and culture regarding healthcare and self-care affect employee hiring, retention, and the bottom line.

As a result, many employers are addressing the well-being of their employees in more meaningful ways, such as through people-centered built environments and wellness programs.

THE SCIENCE OF PHYSICAL SPACE

In recent years, neuroscience has yielded considerable insights into how the immune system can be experimentally suppressed or enhanced through intervention. Our emotional state is connected to our entire being, and our thoughts influence our physiology. What we perceive and how we cope with our perceptions are dictated by messages sent from the brain to the rest of the body.

Leveraging the mind-body connection can have profound results in the healthcare setting. Research by Kiecolt-Glaser and colleagues suggests that less-stressful hospital experiences might result in speedier recovery times at home; that physical comfort in the hospital setting might reduce mortality and morbidity; and that patients in comfortable settings might require fewer narcotic pain medications, experience less anxiety and depression, and suffer fewer postsurgical complications.[3] A hospital experience that is less stressful and more comfortable can also yield higher patient satisfaction, which could in turn result in better compliance with prescribed drug regimens and recommended postsurgical care, including follow-up visits, which can potentially improve clinical outcomes.[4]

If you examined the ways in which this research is being applied to the building of PCEs, you would find that innovation abounds. For example, Delos, a wellness real-estate and technology firm, offers employers certification-based ways to apply health and wellness principles to the design, construction, and operation of indoor environments. Delos pioneered the evidence-based WELL Building Standard that encompasses seven categories of building performance, addressed through features tied to their impact on the human body's major systems (cardiovascular, immune, endocrine, integumentary, muscular, nervous, urinary, skeletal, respiratory, digestive, and reproductive). The categories are:[5]

1   Air (toxic material reduction)

2   Water (fundamental water quality)

3   Nourishment (mindful eating)

4   Light (circadian lighting design)

5   Fitness (active furnishings)

6   Comfort (internally generated noise)

7   Mind (workplace family support)

For example, comfortable, ambient sound levels can be achieved through the strategic use of sound-absorbing materials that reduce reverberation time (providing benefits to the cardiovascular, endocrine, and nervous systems). Planning for natural light can involve such details as accounting for seasons or avoiding excessive amounts of sunlight (benefiting the immune, reproductive, digestive, cardiovascular, nervous, endocrine, and muscular systems). The WELL system's approach, which also aligns with LEED standards, is just one example of keeping the *Healthy Patient* in mind when planning and executing built environments.

THE WELLNESS TREND

When it comes to employer-provided healthcare, there are generally two schools of thought: There are employers invested in their employees' wellness, and they support the programs chosen by their employees, such as by funding a gym membership or contracting wellness services. One example is Calm City, a mobile meditation studio housed in an RV that visits worksites. Then there are those employers who exert greater control over health plan choices and costs. They might institute employee wellness programs but offset the costs by charging more for healthcare for employees who are overweight or who smoke.

Whether the motive is healthcare cost reduction or the desire to live a healthier life, both companies and individuals are increasingly educating themselves on wellness and disease prevention. One advantage for the individual, however, is broadly available, transparent provider information, including statistical and survey data. Patients are basing their health management and medical treatment decisions on treatment costs, alternative medicine options, provider locations, specialties, physical environments, patient testimonials, and reputations, all of which can be researched online or custom delivered by such organizations as The Leapfrog Group, a nonprofit watchdog group that provides data on hospitals, including patient satisfaction and safety data. Patients are also relying on social media to obtain feedback about high-quality, affordable care.

The ability to "shop around" makes a patient essentially no different from any other customer. Nevertheless, because healthcare is about delivering an intimate service experience, a healthcare system needs to carefully consider how it attracts and subsequently satisfies its customer base.

Orchestrating the consumer experience is the subject of Joseph Pine and James Gilmore's book, *The Experience Economy*, which puts forth that every business is a stage, and that the healthcare setting is but another opportunity to manage details in a way that bonds a patient to a healthcare system's brand. What makes the prospect of patient loyalty especially noteworthy is that healthcare service can be intangible and complex, and so patients—who are generally less knowledgeable about healthcare than their providers—might assign added weight to data they can understand, such as firsthand experiences with navigating a healthcare environment or interacting with staff.

There are optimal ways in which to deal with this reality. Leonard L. Berry and colleagues wrote about three categories of clues (functional, mechanic, and humanic) that patients perceive, and which dictate whether a service experience is seen as being a good one or a bad one for them. "When interacting with a system of care, patients filter clues, organizing them into a set of impressions. ... Well-managed clues can evoke positive feelings, such as trust and hope. Poorly managed clues can exacerbate negative emotions, such as anxiety, stress, helplessness, anger, and fear. ... Clue management requires ongoing investment in qualitatively understanding the service experience from the patient's perspective—by discovering what that subjective impression currently is and determining what it should be, then closing this gap."[6]

It makes sense to then suppose that if healthcare institutions can manage the verbal and nonverbal clues of their environments in ways that create positive patient service experiences, they can also touch the hearts and minds of patients and more likely gain their loyalty. Applying this golden rule to the design and build of PCEs therefore requires adopting a *Healthy Patient* mindset.

But I Am Not a Touchy-Feely Manager!

Your primary role as project manager is to meet your original charge: Deliver a PCE that is healing, comforting, safe, protective, and addresses a need or problem. Your approach to planning, designing, and executing the space must also include a holistic component that acknowledges the inextricable connections among the mind, body, and spirit. To do this, you must understand how people experience physical environments through all five senses.

For some people, the term "touchy-feely" has a negative connotation and is a state of mind to be avoided—a code term for situations, thoughts, or actions laden with emotion, such as personal experiences and relationships, trust building, showing compassion, or being affected by sickness or pain and suffering. That said, welcome to today's healthcare, a business rife with emotion and holism unfolding in settings where we now treat not just the physical symptoms of a person's disease, but the entire person.

Believe it or not, you as a project manager have a major role to play in *Healthy Patient*. You might consider your leadership and project tasks as being limited—or that you are but a mere cog in the healthcare system—but this could not be further from the truth. What you decide to do and how you do it, and the space that is ultimately generated as a result, will influence the mental, physical, and spiritual states of the patients, families, staff, and others who will use the PCE. Imagine it being you, or someone you care about, who might enter it one day. What would be your personal hope, worries, or expectations? They would likely not differ markedly from those of anyone else.

You might tell yourself, "This is not about me. I am just here to get things done." But it *is* about you. Your approach to project management must be a personal one, and no matter how discomfited or even challenged you might feel at the thought of uncovering and applying your own perspectives to your management approach, you must bypass such feelings and view the project from a higher vantage point. In other words, to achieve what matters most for an optimal PCE, you must assume a personal stake in the outcome.

The need to go beyond blueprints and sheetrock might seem to you as an added burden on your project plate, but understanding patient motivations, emotions, and desires is imperative for setting the right tone for a project early on. Personal accountability will positively inform every idea that you generate, responsibility that you delegate, and problem that you encounter during each phase of a project to keep you on target. It will also authenticate your leadership and bolster your efforts to guide your team. When you commit to being all in on a project, you will be backing your team members by inspiring, motivating, and supporting them to participate fully and confidently in the project.

MAKING SENIOR MANAGEMENT HAPPY, TOO

All that you do as project manager for a PCE will also translate back to the institution at large. By applying the principle of *Healthy Patient* (recognizing people's need for respect, autonomy, and a supportive, caring environment) to every project phase from initial planning to ribbon cutting, you will stay true to your motivation and desire for better patient outcomes and therefore be more likely to succeed. Medical staff will be able to perform their jobs with greater ease and empowerment, thanks to having participated in a project that focused on the patient. Higher patient-satisfaction survey scores will reflect greater patient trust and loyalty and ultimately result in a better bottom line for the healthcare system. Finally, the delivery of the best possible healthcare will benefit the community at large, as well as society as a whole, making it a win-win for everyone.

The Role of Structure and Process in Healthy Patient

There are two powerful influencers of how patient-centered care is delivered, and you might not have stopped long enough in your day-to-day work to consider their true impact. They are structure and process. Structure (how environments are set up) and process (the healthcare-based workflow and the way in which medical decisions and tasks are carried out) add value to an environment and, in evidence-based areas concerning regulation, ensure public safety for patients and medical professionals alike.

Imagine being a patient arriving at a hospital that had no paved roads, sidewalks, or signage. What if there were no rules or policies available on patient care? What would a patient think or feel? Or what if a nurse encountered a nursing station or exam room that was not properly set up in a manner consistent with accepted protocols, or if critical medical supplies, medications, or equipment were stored in random locations? How could work possibly proceed in a professional and safe manner in the absence of proper structure?

Now imagine being an outside vendor, architect, engineer, or construction manager assigned to design and build a hospital waiting room or triage center. With no established standards or workflow processes and protocols or information on existing mechanical systems, you might feel as if you were in the Wild West.

The provision of healthcare in general is driven by structure and process, and because these influencers underpin a project, there is always room for improvement. Several organizations, including the Association of Healthcare Engineers, The Center for Health Design, Planetree, the Robert Wood Johnson Foundation, the International WELL Building Institute, and the U.S. Green Building Council (LEED), offer education on implementing best practices and improving processes for healthcare facilities. A wealth of continually updated information exists regarding rules, standards, and supporting resources, making it necessary for a project manager to stay on top of the latest developments while maintaining efficiency.

DEVELOPING PCE-SPECIFIC PROTOCOLS

I fell into project management because it felt natural to me. Managing chaos was something I did well. I have always been a fixer. My teaching skills helped me transition to my current field more easily, and over time I developed a management style of trusting my gut on matters that are not necessarily black and white and tackling challenges armed with a sense of humor.

In contrast, most project managers are very process-oriented, which is why the *Project Management Body of Knowledge (PMBOK)* guide is the industry's standard reference and the bible for so many professionals, and for good reason. However, in the context of healthcare project management, *PMBOK* did not provide me with the depth of coverage and guidance that I needed for planning and executing PCE projects.

This was a critical gap for me, especially since I was in the midst of learning more about the personal nature of healing. I needed to move beyond what already existed and develop structure and process protocols that worked in my project management world. This motivated me to return to school in 2007 to pursue a master's degree in integrative health and healing. Integrative medicine is a rapidly growing field that addresses wellness and illness from a holistic perspective. It involves comparing, connecting, and integrating conventional, alternative, and complementary approaches to promote health and wellness, as well as healing and prevention. Importantly, integrative medicine puts patients first. Patients and providers partner to treat the "whole patient" through a diagnostic and therapeutic program that draws from different medical traditions, specialties, and modalities.

I felt very strongly that if I were to embark on creating hospital-based PCEs, I had to approach healthcare in a way that reflects the increasing shift of it being "disease driven" to being focused on safeguarding health. The opportunity to do this came when I and two fellow graduate students, Germaine and Kathy, collaborated on a culminating project while working at Stamford Hospital in Connecticut. We decided that since, at the time, most healthcare systems were unfamiliar with integrative medicine centers and few protocols existed for creating them, we would develop a "how-to" manual for introducing an integrative medicine center into a hospital environment. We felt strongly that such a tool was much needed, particularly since the medical community was not yet fully on board with the idea of integrative medicine.

We knew that to succeed we needed to keep our ideas simple and pool our respective strengths and experiences. Germaine was a nurse, whose many credentials included expertise in alternative modalities. She served as our editor and also developed the manual's protocols. My background was in business planning and strategy, marketing, and construction project management, and so I developed those aspects of the manual. Kathy, also a nurse, had a background in integrative medicine and alternative therapies, and she managed the research and indexing in addition to her own writing.

As we conceived and then outlined the manual, we kept returning to the same question: How could we write a well-organized, easy-to-understand manual without compromising our guiding principles or having users drown in a sea of information? To keep ourselves razor-focused and accountable to the powers that be, we established a hard-and-fast research timeline. We brainstormed on structure and process. We visited other U.S. integrative medicine centers to learn about their patient populations, about the communities they served (including the medical community), and how they generated revenue.

During the writing phase, we adhered strictly to four guiding principles for building an integrative medicine center:

1   A healthcare system should be designed in a way that supports a whole-person philosophy (that accounts for the body, mind, and spirit) and serves a diverse population.

2   The best of conventional medicine and proven alternative healing practices can be co-delivered directly to individuals who prefer taking an integrative approach to their healing.

3   The concept of a patient self-care/expert medical care partnership and a collaborative healthcare team approach are integral to delivering optimal healthcare.

4   A successful design vision is one that illustrates and supports an environment conducive to healing yet offers advanced wellness technologies.

The final manual, titled, *Integrative Medicine Program Proposal for a Hospital Setting,* supported this new direction in healthcare, bringing patient care closer to what we value and understand about wellness and self-empowerment in the health continuum. It showed users how to create an elegant and functional space, in which both patients and staff could collaborate, learn, and plan holistic patient-centered care to support healing the whole person.

To offer readers, including our professors, a practical taste of the structure and process of a PCE built on the guiding principles set forth in the manual, we included a rendering that served as a virtual "walkthrough" of an ideally designed PCE, as seen from a user's perspective. It is worth including here a narrative based on this rendering to illustrate the potential outcome of applying the principle of *Healthy Patient* to a project.

Imagine that you are a patient visiting a newly built PCE for the first time. Upon entering the environment, you find yourself walking through a nature setting featuring lush, fragrant gardens that infuse the space with vibrant color and a sense of (secular) spirituality. The atmosphere feels timeless and is filled with sights and sounds chosen for their connection to wood, fire, earth, metal, and water, the five traditional elements associated with Chinese medicine that form the basis for the cyclical relationship between the physiology of the human body and the natural world.

Crossing the threshold of the reception area, you step onto a bamboo floor and hear the serene sounds of a waterfall.

An attentive receptionist sitting at a curved desk guides you to a refreshment area for water or tea. You sit down in an open space designed to facilitate conversation, taking in the plush carpeting, fresh flowers, and metal bamboo sculptures. The calming scent of lavender emanating from electric candles, along with elegant ceiling draping, helps you center your thoughts and settle into an atmosphere of calm energy, a relaxed but focused state of reduced stress that readies you for a more engaging consultation with your medical professional.

This representative healing environment, aligned with the hospital's core values, elicited positive reactions and feedback from the participants and proved indispensable in helping us further refine our design principles. Because we had taken an extra *Healthy Patient* step, the manual could serve as a resource for creating an elegant, functional integrative medicine center, in which patients and staff could learn, collaborate, and plan patient care to allow healing to take place.

BUILDING AN INTEGRATIVE MEDICINE CENTER

The manual's walkthrough, the result of countless hours of research by Germaine, Kathy, and myself, was an extremely valuable exercise regarding my own professional life. A year after its completion, and shortly after I graduated and was still working at Stamford Hospital, I was assigned to build the Center for Integrative Medicine & Wellness at the Tully Health Center (an ambulatory care facility). Lucky for me, I had my indispensable manual at my disposal to assist in conceptualizing, designing, and building the center, including determining the use of space, the criteria for choosing design elements, the types of education areas that would be set up, and the workflow processes.

In addition to relying on the manual, I worked to tap into the culture of preventive care and wellness that the hospital had already established for its community, and which was based on the Planetree philosophy of patient-centered care. Planetree emphasizes the delivery of care in a manner that works best for patients, recognizing that the patient is an individual to be cared for, not a medical condition to be treated. Each patient is unique with different needs, knowledge, and expertise regarding their care. Above all is the recognition that patients know their bodies best.

The nine formal elements that underlie Planetree patient-centered care are:[7]

1   The importance of human interaction

2   Informing and empowering diverse populations (consumer health libraries and patient education)

3   Healing partnerships (the importance of including family and friends)

4   Nutrition (the nurturing aspects of food)

5   Spirituality (inner resources for healing)

6   Human touch (the essentials of communicating caring through massage)

7   Healing arts (nutrition for the soul)

8   Integrating complementary and alternative practices into conventional care

9   Healing environments (architecture and design conducive to health)

To reflect Planetree elements and *Healthy Patient* principles in the project, patients receiving outpatient and inpatient care at the center would be informed by educational resources that stressed integrative medicine modalities. Meanwhile, the broader patient population—members of the community and healthcare professionals themselves—would be targeted with outreach programs designed to attract patients and educate them on the features and benefits of a combined conventional and alternative medicine approach.

Working in our favor was that most potential patients were familiar with paying out of pocket for alternative therapies. Since the center accepted many insurance plans, including plans managed by the hospital, we could reach a larger portion of the local community and perhaps even win over more of the skeptics.

Since the Center for Integrative Medicine & Wellness would be the first center of its kind in Fairfield County, we wanted its design to communicate three important things: the types of integrative services offered, the idea that preventive care and wellness could be addressed through a combination of modalities, and that benefits could be achieved through a positive, memorable, and more personal healing experience that began the moment a patient entered the space. Simply put, we set out to tell a story that integrative medicine was a viable option for a person's journey to wellness. But doing so required a carefully considered strategy for the center's structure (the built environment itself).

The challenges we faced were not insignificant. The hospital's marketing and human resources departments had to work in tandem to position the center as a provider of preventive services, not just a place to rush to when something went wrong (a job for marketing), as well as integrate the center's services with the hospital's existing employee wellness program (which fell under human resources).

Another challenge was convincing the hospital administration about the benefits of offering patients an integrative medicine option. Decision makers were stuck in the mindset that alternative therapies were boutique services, and this attitude did not begin to shift until a donor stepped in with a generous gift to cover the project's design, construction, and start-up costs. Eventually, the administration realized that aligning conventional medical services and alternative therapies was possible, although what sealed the deal was buy-in from the local community and the assurance that the center would generate revenue.

As we planned out the center's physical environment, we forged connections with the community. One simple yet powerful way to do this was to take our design cues from local natural landscapes. Inspired by Stamford's beautiful downtown area located right on Long Island Sound, as well as by the rolling hills and lakes and ponds of neighboring North Stamford, we worked to bring the outdoors indoors.

Patients who visit the Center for Integrative Medicine & Wellness today enter an open, calming space designed with a coastal theme. In the waiting area are a soothing water wall, relaxing music, and an offering of herbal teas. A receptionist warmly greets patients and checks them in, after which they are escorted to a changing room and given a soft spa-quality robe and comfortable plush slippers. The waiting room is reassuringly private and secure, and if patients need to go elsewhere for X-rays or other diagnostic tests, they will not have to travel far or change back into street clothes.

Patients who must visit another waiting area will encounter coordinated design elements that reflect balance, harmony, and rhythm at every turn. Walls are lined with beautiful artwork featuring serene landscapes to distract the worried mind. To keep noise levels down, the waiting areas and exam rooms are located away from the staff offices and workroom.

No one is left out of consideration. While patients receive care, the staff works in an office environment designed to promote productivity and well-being. A specially designed group room facilitates collaborative learning and patient care planning. And when they need to unwind and recharge during the workday, these dedicated, caring professionals can also care for themselves by taking advantage of a lounge that serves as a quiet retreat.

POST-PROJECT ANALYSIS

Conceiving and creating an elegant, highly functional space in which patients and staff can collaborate, learn, and experience high-quality patient care that promotes healing takes substantial research, including inpatient and outpatient site visits. We as a team were passionate about building a center that represented a new model for healthcare, and we thought carefully about how to facilitate the delivery of care for patients and support for medical staff.

Understanding why the Center for Integrative Medicine & Wellness had a successful opening and continues to be a highly respected and well-run center requires going beyond the surface of its set up (the project's goals, approach, patients served, administration's involvement, etc.) to examine how the "yin-yang" of structure and process resulted in a PCE that answers the needs of both patients and staff. Looking back, it is easy to spot the contributing factors.

Throughout the project, we relied on the virtues of simplicity and open-mindedness. We tried not to sacrifice our overarching project vision by losing ourselves in the minutiae of countless tasks, and we maintained a willingness to learn and apply lessons learned at every turn. We assumed nothing and never uttered the words, "We always do it this way." We might not have had all the answers, but we did know how to focus on *Healthy Patient* guiding principles, which helped push away our doubts.

I cannot emphasize enough how our efforts were supported by the hospital's adherence to the Planetree model of patient care. Many of our team members were unfamiliar with complementary medicine, which could have posed a significant problem, but with a hospital culture of wellness already in place we had the creative license to roll out our ideas for the design of the center's workflow.

What also informed team members were stories that I shared about my visits to other centers, which helped members visualize the new center through follow-up conversations led by the question, "What if?" It was critical not to rush this exploratory phase. Before we thought of design schematics, we spent six weeks brainstorming, holding focused discussions, conducting research, formulating theories, and sharing opinions. These activities ignited the team's passion for building a center that would better people's lives.

Another great advantage for us was having the confidence and support of hospital leadership. We had a physician champion on our team who inspired confidence and gave us the credibility we needed to connect like-minded people in the community who would support us. We also gained the full backing and confidence of the hospital administration and obtained approvals by never overselling concepts and by communicating ideas through presentations and pitch decks that effectively justified our design requests, particularly for ideas that would change the status quo. We used this creative freedom to establish a signature brand for the center that tied back to the main hospital through subtle, tasteful treatments of signage, millwork, soap dispensers, and other branding opportunities.

As with any project, our team had its ups and downs regarding presentations and approvals. Not everyone accepted our ideas, and the center itself became a sore point with some local physicians who did not believe in alternative modalities. But if simplicity is a virtue, so is tenacity. If the administration categorically rejected an idea, we would not just forget about it. Instead, we discussed the nature of the objections and proposed a revised idea, exercising patience and giving people time to mull over the ideas and discuss them with others. By doing our homework and following up, we changed minds and got the approvals we needed to move forward.

Throughout the entire project, I served as the facilitator, working with administration to implement changes or finding ways to supply my team with the tools, resources, and information they needed. One of the best lessons I learned—perhaps the most important step in setting up our process—was the need to trust my team members and make it easy for them to succeed. Our team knew what it wanted to accomplish, and as its leader I had to prioritize for what was best for the patients and staff. I often stepped back and let others take the lead and apply their unique experiences to the task at hand. I also made sure to schedule enough time for brainstorming and collaboration, which are essential for coming up with great ideas and strengthening team bonds.

In the end, we had built one of the first successful integrative medicine centers in Fairfield County, both in functionality and in cost-effectiveness (the center became profitable within three years of its opening). The process that we instituted for taking the project from start to finish garnered much positive feedback. This was greatly satisfying to me as the project manager; however, the experience also showed me how, in those early years, we had only touched the tip of the iceberg regarding how a PCE could be "well done" by respecting and applying the principles of *Healthy Patient*.

An Understanding of Healing and a Balance of Process

Let us step back from the practical interplay of structure and process to examine the importance and impact of two inextricably linked ideas underlying the three pillars of *Health Well Done* (*Healthy Patient*, *Healthy Team*, and *Healthy Project*), but which apply most directly to a *Healthy Patient* mindset. To successfully adopt a holistic people-centric outlook instead of a strictly process outlook for a PCE project, the entire team must commit to operating with an "understanding of healing" while maintaining a "balance of process."

UNDERSTANDING OF HEALING

Every patient is on his or her own personal journey of healing. Having an understanding of healing means being clear on, and sensitive to, what a patient needs and expects of a healthcare institution from a holistic, emotional perspective. This understanding is the touchstone that guides a team during project initiation and early planning stages, as members gather, interpret, and manage information that can include statistical data, anecdotes, project history, institutional resources, staff attitudes and wisdom, C-suite expectations, and patient experiences.

For example, when I shared my cancer diagnosis with my family, my brother and cousin urged me to visit New York City hospitals for second opinions and treatment. But I was sold on Stamford Hospital because my treatment plan there would consist of chemotherapy along with alternative medicine, yoga, massage, reiki, craniosacral therapy, art therapy, healing through sound, a personal trainer for three months, and a gym membership for six months. I knew that Stamford Hospital was the right fit because of its integrative medicine approach and because I had researched what other hospitals were offering. I was not a big fan of going into the city for treatment, despite people telling me that I would receive better care there. I educated myself, followed my treatment plan, and envisioned myself skiing on Christmas day. This is what got me through the treatments and back to being myself.

This personal anecdote illustrates one of two critical messages that must be embraced to gain an understanding of healing. The first is that the concept of healing is not the same for everyone. Every patient experiences his or her care in a different way. Patients are not a homogenous cohort of sick people, but rather unique humans with personalities, preferences, responsibilities, dreams, wisdom, and experiences. It matters not whether the patient diagnosed with cancer is a tech giant or a kindergarten teacher. Both must embark on a difficult journey that, among other challenges, will include the loss of control. A CEO of a start-up might go from leading teams of professionals to needing teams of professionals to do the smallest things, such as get into a chair or take a shower. Putting yourself in another person's shoes provides insight for developing a clear intention and vision, a focus on priorities, and the resolve to stay the course despite challenges and roadblocks.

The second, equally important message is that the evolution of preventive care will profoundly influence how structure and process are considered in future PCEs, making it even more necessary to think proactively about patient needs throughout the project, not only regarding the treatment of illness but the support and promotion of wellness, such as through patient education.

For example, many patients came to the Center for Integrative Medicine & Wellness after unsuccessful attempts to lose weight or manage pain. We decided to make full use of the center's herb garden by offering a cooking lab, where patients could learn how to prepare healthful meals using fresh herbs. Our goal was to help people tackle their everyday struggles in managing their health by exposing them to an educational environment that could support their efforts to eat better or to manage pain and stress.

A commitment to proactively considering patient needs ensures that no matter how the healthcare industry evolves, structure and process will always be patient centered. Although we can never know everything about the experiential process of healing, we can still strive to achieve an understanding of healing by maintaining a compassionate and open mind.

BALANCE OF PROCESS

When an understanding of healing is adopted by the entire team, the work of creating the structure of the environment—the process, and the backbone of a *Healthy Project*—can be more comprehensive and efficient and thereby successful. A balance of process reflects a never-ending consideration of the "people aspects" and organizational culture behind a project. Proper vigilance requires juggling all the project variables without sacrificing the priorities associated with delivering high-quality patient care. Achieving a balance of process sets the stage for an efficient, patient-centered process in the newly built environment.

Having balance does not mean sacrificing the welfare or efforts of your team. Regardless of the caliber of your technical skills, as a healthcare project manager you are de facto in the people business, and so must you look after your team by applying your "soft skills"—those managerial skills used to motivate and encourage a team on an interpersonal level—to offset the heavier managerial tasks of enforcing rules and processes. Sometimes this means sitting back and letting people resolve issues on their own, while at other times it calls for practicing active leadership by stepping in and taking control of a situation.

Finally, establishing a balance of process in your project will pay great dividends in ensuring clear modes of communication, encouraging innovation in PCE operations and workflows, and helping you manage the budget and schedule. It will empower team members to be focused, productive, and caring. It will also accommodate their collective wisdom, experience, and patient-centered philosophy, allowing these positive qualities to be reflected in the final physical environment. Luckily, process can be guided by the principles of *Healthy Project,* which is covered in Chapter 3.

A Tale of Two Fish Tanks

A balance of process benefits every detail of a PCE project that adheres to a *Healthy Patient* philosophy, whether that detail is large or small—even as seemingly innocuous as an aquarium accent. But the road to equilibrium can vary, as the following two examples of aquarium installations will show.

The act of watching fish in an aquarium, even for 5 minutes, can be significantly restorative. Research by Deborah Cracknell and colleagues revealed that, "aquariums may trigger physiological, as well as psychological responses, that are indicative of calming and stress-reducing effects," including the potential for increased relaxation and positive mood, as well as a lowering of heart rate and blood pressure.[8] It was no surprise to me, therefore, when an emergency room staff requested to have an aquarium set up in the children's corner of their waiting room.

After the idea was approved, we hired a local pet store that specialized in aquariums to make a presentation on equipment needs, design options, and fish selection. In the meantime, the infection prevention nurse, along with environmental service director, drafted a "fish tank policy" that outlined water purification procedures for the tank, the installation of locks on cabinets, and the responsibilities for feeding the fish, stocking supplies, and maintaining the tank.

The second fish tank scenario (part of a later project) involved installing an aquarium in a cardiologist's office. As proposed by the physician, however, the tank would have been sited in such a way that patients could peer through it to see the cardiologist sitting at his desk, but they would have their backs to the tank once they sat down, thus defeating the purpose of an aquarium. Despite this obvious "structure" flaw, the physician was adamant about his chosen location. Our team discussed the fish tank policy, maintenance costs, and care responsibilities with the office manager and staff, who ultimately did not want to commit to having an office aquarium, and so the proposal was scrapped.

Here are two fish tales with different outcomes, yet both cases can be considered successful from a project management perspective. How so? In both situations we followed the same process: We identified the challenge, found a solution (while meeting compliance and budgetary requirements), maintained open lines of communication with the staff, and put people first by letting the staff decide what was best for their patients and themselves regarding an environmental change. With regard to the emergency room aquarium, the staff was having fun designing the tank and had committed to the requirements of the fish tank policy, and so we wound up focused less on policy and more on the staff and the young beneficiaries of a relaxing aquatic scene.

At the cardiologist's office, we had to ask ourselves, "Are we serving patients by locating the tank in the physician's office?" Given the proposed location of the tank, we knew the answer to the question. However, we also respected the reticence of the office staff to accept the work and expense involved in following the stringent fish tank policy. In the end, we knew the right decision for all concerned was to not set up a tank in the cardiologist's office.

Meeting Patients Where They Are

Keep in mind that even highly engaged patients spend most of their time outside the medical setting simply living their everyday lives. Since the support of an individual's lifelong health and well-being cannot be limited to any one setting, we must ask ourselves how PCE structure and process can be determined in ways that

HEALTH WELL DONE

account for the many other influencers on people's efforts to manage their overall health and well-being.

Earlier in this chapter we touched on the concept of a culture of health that is a continuum of our overall health and well-being, whether it is present in our homes, schools, offices, or other settings outside the typical healthcare environment. Specifically, healthcare providers must meet patients where they live, work, and play—physically and virtually, such as on smartphones—even as, paradoxically, healthcare becomes more personalized. For example, millennials have grown up expecting that almost everything can be done in real time and conveniently online. The trend for instant gratification is here to stay and requires automated systems that can serve patients by providing information or allowing them to set up appointments, for example.

This is just one of many considerations that you will face in your efforts to manage PCE projects. The good news is that you need not have all the answers to the concerns that arise as you strive to build truly holistic PCEs. But you will be more assured of success if you remember to do two things: Remain committed to the principles of *Healthy Patient* despite the healthcare industry's push toward reducing costs, and do not underestimate the powerful role that structure and process play in the delivery of patient-centered care.

Never Forget the Healthcare Professionals

Healthcare professionals are both scientific and deeply passionate about their work, which is another reason why it is important to prioritize for *Healthy Patient* by addressing the needs of the

46

heart, mind, and spirit of all stakeholders. Too often, teams that deliver medical services are overwhelmed and lack the resources to provide a high-quality, efficient patient experience. Unfortunately, absent a proven method to apply toward that goal, team members might not connect with a patient's emotional side and become more in touch with themselves in the process. One highly effective way to connect is through storytelling. Stories that feature real-life characters and events can be mined for lessons and ideas regarding the patient experience (see Chapter 4, "The Art of Storytelling"). Storytelling both feeds and frees the human spirit and helps connect a professional's brilliant mind to their passionate heart. It is the miraculous combination of these core aspects of our humanity—heart, mind, and spirit—that helps explain the seemingly endless supply of comfort, compassion, and empathy that healthcare professionals provide their patients.

From a project's start, it is critical to hear from these stakeholders—technicians, nurses, doctors, front-desk staff, and other key personnel—who are already living their professional lives by the code of Healthy Patient. Their insights, wisdom, and experiences can guide your team as you plan, design, and build the environment in which they will care for their patients.

Above all, always keep the bigger picture in mind. Understanding healing and achieving a balance of process under the guidance of Healthy Patient, Healthy Team, and Healthy Project will set you on the path to success. When drama hits—whether about scheduling pressures or budget cuts—just focus on establishing this foundation and you will finish the project having prioritized for the needs of patients and medical professionals. Remember, too, that your success will have a positive impact on a healthcare system's brand identity and the even greater goal of contributing to the well-being of all Americans.

NUTS AND BOLTS

How can you as a project leader bolster your collective efforts to design novel PCEs in practical ways that support *Healthy Patient* priorities?

Lead with Your Heart, Mind, and Spirit

Allowing your humanity to be up front and center during a project might not be the easiest shift to make in a typical management approach, but it is a worthwhile one and will come easier and more intuitive to you with time. Tapping into a wellspring of insights by recognizing stakeholder needs will help you execute practical patient-centric tasks.

 HELPFUL TIPS

[1]   **Keep your eye on the big picture.** Remember that we are all connected. Winston Churchill was right when he said, "Healthy citizens are our best asset."

[2]   **Employ a patient-centered strategy.** Find out early in the project process whether the healthcare system you are serving has a patient-centered strategy (the Planetree model of care is one example) and let it inform all project phases. If no such strategy exists, develop one with your team using *Healthy Patient* as a guide. It will be time and money well spent. Keep it simple to better motivate everyone.

[3]   **Become a touchy-feely project manager.** You can then lead by example. The more you practice it, the more naturally it will come to you.

[4]   **Use storytelling whenever and wherever you can.** Storytelling makes conversations more productive. You and your team can apply the valuable lessons that emerge from the act of sharing experiences to benefit the project.

[5]   **Strongly encourage the use of key skills.** Your *Healthy Team* can benefit from adopting a compassion-based perspective that reflects a willingness to collaborate and be open to innovative thinking.

[6]   **Remember that experience is your teacher.** Heed the wisdom of your *Healthy Team* when building an environment that many team members will occupy.

Teach Your Team to Think Like a Healthy Patient

Embracing the principles of *Healthy Patient* requires good intentions on the part of all project participants. To help reinforce open-mindedness and creativity and keep you on track with all this touchy-feely stuff, here are questions to ask of yourself and the team, simple exercises, and management actions to help everyone learn more about patient needs.

QUESTIONS TO ASK

Do we all have an understanding of healing?

How can we help patients who visit the PCE feel normal, in control, and focused on their care and treatment?

How can we give patients the appropriate physical resources they need (for example, alternative seating, private spaces, working areas, and a place to be educated)?

 EXERCISES

[1]   **To appreciate what is important in life:** Have everyone close their eyes and imagine how their everyday existence would be affected if they were unable to accomplish even the simplest of tasks, such as wash their hands, reach for an elevator button, or use a bathroom on their own.

[2]   **To inspire thoughts of happiness:** Have the team relax and concentrate on their breathing. Ask them to picture their favorite color. (Color has the power to alter a person's mood.) Do they see a correlation between color and happiness? Does it make them smile? Does it evoke any memories? What three things first come to mind? Does the color remind them of a person, a moment in time, or a cherished possession?

[3] **To understand how patients subconsciously determine their confidence level in the medical services they will receive:** Count from one to seven. Then do it again, but this time pay closer attention to everything around you. (Seven seconds is about the average time it takes to form an opinion about an environment.) Since patients might arrive at an environment already feeling stressed, the littlest thing can make them feel more anxious, frustrated, and challenged. Balance your efforts for creating an efficient work area and enabling metric-driven results (like turnaround times) with a staff's need to provide patient-centered care.

[4] **To understand that we learn best in group settings:** With team members broken out into pairs, have one person sketch out on paper a problem situation for a waiting room and ask the other person to explain what he or she sees. Do both people view the problem similarly or not? Can they come up with a solution to the problem?

[5] **To understand why integrative medicine is the future of healthcare:** Set up two blank flip charts. On the first chart, have team members write down ways to treat a patient with diabetes from a conventional medicine approach. On the second chart, have them list alternative treatments, such as massage, guided imagery, yoga, herbs, nutrition, and supplements. Then have the team review both charts and create a combined treatment plan. Talk through the benefits of the new plan in terms of cost, better outcomes, better connections through high-touch modalities, and preventive healthcare.

HELPFUL TIPS

[1] **Keep information flow simple.** In the sea of PCE complexity, too much theory and research can bog you down.

[2] **Ask medical stakeholders plenty of questions.** Tap into the expertise of the professionals who specialize in the disease or medical field to be treated in the PCE. Asking them about their workflow processes, patient interactions, challenges they face, and what they would like to change about their environment will help you prioritize for specific needs.

   For example, for a pulmonary disease department, will the distance from the entranceway to a waiting area or receptionist desk account for patients who have trouble walking, such as with seating every 300 feet? Are the design colors for an environment being carefully considered? (Although blue is almost universally seen as a calming color, other colors might have cultural connotations that should be considered given a practice's patient population.)

[3] **Involve staff at the front lines.** Do not forget about the many people who deal directly with patient arrival and discharge activities and protocols, including the parking attendant, the front-desk person, and hospital volunteers to the nurses and other personnel. (*See* Resources, page 293.)

[4] **Talk with families and caretakers.** Uncover what these important patient care partners need (such as ways to keep a hospital room clean and disinfected).

[5] **Know where to go for questions on standards and compliance.** Do not overlook this important aspect of project management. The following organizations are great for this information: American Society for Healthcare Engineering (ASHE); Facility Guidelines Institute (FGI); The Center for Health Design (CHD); American Hospital Association (AHA), and your state health department's office of regulatory planning.

[6] **Follow the money.** Be clear on how a health system is compensated to be sure that there is money in your budget. Also find out if you must set up separate cost centers.

[7] **Never hesitate to ask for help.** One of the advantages of working with a *Healthy Team* is being able to lean on team members and benefit from everyone's real-world wisdom and experience.

[8] **Remain curious about best practices and the future of patient care.** Educate yourself on the latest PCE research and on revisions to Centers for Medicare and Medicaid Services (CMS) policies and the Affordable Care Act (ACA); subscribe to industry publications, including *Healthcare Design, Health Facilities Management, H&HN,* and *Inside ASHE;* tap into professional management groups; and attend conferences, such as the Healthcare Design Expo and events held by ASHE and Planetree.

Conclusion

This chapter on *Healthy Patient* has set up the "why" of your PCE project, providing you with the principles that will constantly remind you of the importance of the patient-provider relationship, the need to respect the heart, mind, and spirit, and the fact that every person's healing journey is unique. Fully embracing the *Healthy Patient* mindset, while also recognizing the need for an understanding of healing and balance of process, will help you and your team develop the purpose and passion needed to make the right decisions in the design, planning, and building of a PCE.

Now that you have a north star to follow, let us move on to Chapter 2, where I delve more deeply into what makes a great project manager and how to build a productive and motivated *Healthy Team* to ensure that your *Healthy Project* succeeds.

KEY TAKEAWAYS

- Remember that *Healthy Patient* is the reason for all the budgeting, planning, and building of a PCE.

- The PCE that you build should reflect and support an active partnership between the patient and the clinician.

- Your approach to project management should reflect a personal stake in the outcome of the PCE.

- A highly functional space will promote healing.

- Throughout every phase of the project, rely on the virtues of simplicity and open-mindedness, and have them reflected in the PCE.

- Trust your team members and make it easy for them to succeed.

- Find ways to support and guide your project team, including with tools, resources, and information that can improve their performance.

- Help your team commit to operating with an "understanding of healing" while maintaining a "balance of process."

- When using a process-driven approach, balance it with the need to account for the human element.

HEALTHY TEAM

CHAPTER 2

"Coming together is a beginning.
Keeping together is progress.
Working together is success."

— Henry Ford

Healthy Team is the component of *Health Well Done* that ideally describes a group of professionals who work together under a shared understanding of their project's vision and scope and of the culture that underlies an institution and its people. The *Harvard Business Review* is right in saying, "The heart of any project, and the true engine of its work, is its membership."[1] This is why bringing together the right people is extremely important.

A *Healthy Team* has an appointed project leader and is surrounded by representatives of finance, real estate, architecture, engineering, construction, furniture and equipment departments, building services, as well as by doctors, nurses, and other hospital staff. The project leader must cultivate a culture of trust within the team to facilitate communication, collaboration, and accountability, and to ensure that each participant's point of view is fairly considered. A group that functions under a common intention can collaborate effectively to complete a *Healthy Project.*

What Makes a Great Project Manager?

Build projects are more likely to run smoothly and achieve a successful outcome if they are led by individuals with the right people skills, which include the ability to accept and encourage diversity and to understand the need for team members to be heard and to feel important. Before pen even hits paper, you as a project leader must step out of the usual "autopilot" setting of your typical planning style to assess your own strengths, weaknesses, management style, and motivations. Although you do not need to know everything about healthcare to manage a patient-centered healthcare environment (PCE) project, there are powerful leadership traits worth cultivating if you want to bring out the best in yourself and in your *Healthy Team.* It might not be the most comfortable undertaking, but it will yield dividends once you are in the trenches.

FIRST, KNOW THYSELF

Whether building an organization or overseeing a project team, a leader must serve as a coach who inspires, motivates, applies discipline, and keeps everyone on track. Well-known management consultant David C. Baker summarizes his "Top 10 Characteristics of Great Project Managers" by saying, "Great project managers plan, manage, and handle details in a way that lets others relax."[2]

Since it all starts with you, how much do you know about yourself in the context of project leadership? What do you consider to be the traits of successful, productive leaders? Leadership expert and author Jim Collins might surprise you with qualities that are not necessarily what first come to mind for many people. Under his Level 5 Leadership concept, he identifies a seemingly paradoxical duo of traits—humility and professional will—as being necessary for taking an organization from "just good" to "great." Humility stems from dedicating one's ambition to the successful outcome of an effort rather than to one's personal success, and it describes a spirit of service toward family, community, and humanity in general. Professional will, according to Collins, is the "fierce resolve" that no matter what it takes, you will push through the bad times and finish the project.[3]

In other words, being a great leader is not necessarily about being a bold, larger-than-life personality. Collins points to successful Level 5 leaders who are quiet, self-effacing, humble individuals who have taken their companies to great heights. As he puts it, "They are more like Lincoln or Socrates than Patton or Caesar."[4]

If you ask Google's Project Oxygen research team about what defines a great project manager, they will tell you about their data-mining study based on employee surveys, performance appraisals, top manager nominations, and other quantitative and qualitative data that helped them arrive at eight behaviors common among their highest-rated managers.

A great project manager:[5]

1 Is a good coach

2 Empowers the team and does not micromanage

3 Expresses an interest/concern for team members' success and personal well-being

4 Is productive and results oriented

5 Is a good communicator

6 Helps with career development

7 Has a clear vision/strategy for the team

8 Has important technical skills that help him or her advise the team

To this list, I would add a few more traits that I believe are important for effective leadership and are worth discussing:

Open-Mindedness

In my personal interview with her, Becca Nell, a certified project management professional with two decades of consulting experience, told me that being open-minded "is critical if you have compiled a team of talented experts. To have a preconceived notion, or for even any of the team members to be close-minded, it will defy trust and limit the ability of the team to develop a creative solution."[6]

Part of being an open-minded project manager means knowing that you and your team members will bring to the project unique and changeable beliefs, concerns, and needs that will have a tremendous impact on daily work. Emotions, in particular, can affect the workplace. It is sometimes difficult for people to set aside bad feelings, which can have ramifications in an environment where life literally begins and ends, with many critical events occurring in between. Project managers are therefore obligated to not only manage the pace of a project, but to be aware of the mindset of their team members.

For example, during an emergency room renovation I worked on in 2009, a woman had been rushed to the hospital with serious injuries sustained from a chimpanzee attack, which caused a media storm and a security shutdown of the hospital. Many medical professionals found themselves dealing with shock and grief arising from having treated the woman. I needed to set a pace for the project that accommodated the emergency department personnel's need to process their emotions, and so I strategically adjusted the schedule to ease the pressure placed on the staff while keeping the project moving.

Keeping an open mind allows you to make quick, important adjustments to changing circumstances—often on the fly—and shows respect for both the patients whom the organizations is serving and for what your team is bringing to the project.

A Sense of Humor

Cultivating team harmony through humor, applied appropriately, is one of the best ways to alleviate frustration, defuse the blame game, stave off power plays, and keep everyone grounded and you sane. When things are not going according to plan, a sense of humor can put out many firestorms that come your way.

Hurdis Smith, project manager at Sevan Multi-Site Solutions in New York, once told me that my best attribute was my disarming personality. He and I had worked on a renovation project together. He represented the client and I was on the landlord's side. Unfortunately, the landlord's contractor was not meeting schedule milestones, which had a huge impact on the client's schedule. Every week, I would arrive at the project meeting with bad news about a situation out of my control because the landlord would not fire the contractor.

Armed with humor and honesty, I kept everyone on both sides calm and cooperative. They knew that I was genuinely trying to be helpful. Hurdis and I worked together with respect, civility, and professionalism, which allowed the project to be completed more quickly.

Always remember that when working on a team, you are "on stage." People are watching you, and their impression of the type of leader they think you are will be a lasting one. When the time comes to recruit new teams for their next projects, decision makers will more likely seek out your services, having seen firsthand that when the going gets tough, you react calmly and use humor to divert the team from drama to problem solving.

Independent, Focused Thinking

Issues of transparency, compliance, financial risk, schedules, available resources, and team dynamics, among other concerns, can overwhelm a project leader with stress and pressure. Independent thinkers are able to pause long enough to push aside the many distracting "business" aspects of a project to maintain end-result priorities, such as keeping a team inspired and focused on important stakeholders who include patients, families, staff, administration, and security and facilities personnel.

Confidence and Good Self-Esteem

These two characteristics are widely recognized as being important for reducing conflict and creating an environment conducive to productive team relationships. Building a team's confidence starts with you yourself being grounded, present, self-aware, and feeling capable of handling any situation that comes your way.

Self-Care

One way to sustain the energy needed to work on complex projects and feel good about yourself is to set aside time for self-care. This includes looking after your physical health (seeing the doctor or dentist, eating well, exercising) and your emotional health (making time for family and friends, engaging in fun activities and hobbies). Make sure that you carve out true "me time"—time spent by yourself to meditate, read, nap, or take a mind-clearing walk, for example. I highly recommended that you turn off your phone for 20 minutes a day.

My husband is an assistant dean who works one day a week supervising students at a Bronx hospital dental department. Weekend gatherings with students are always eventful at our Vermont home. The days are filled with good company, amazing food, and fun activities. My husband enjoys challenging the students, but he also makes sure to teach them the value of self-care and relaxation. As a gift to them, he will hire a massage therapist to visit the house to provide massages, as well as teach students about the benefits of massage, useful breathing techniques to help with focus, and proper stretching exercises to prevent injuries. By stressing to his students the importance of relaxation and self-care, my husband prepares them for dealing with the busy pace of the dental residency program so that they become better practitioners.

BE A SPECTATOR

The value of having strong observation skills can never be overstated and deserves special mention here. Observation involves more than just collecting information about the world. It is another way of "listening" and, for a project manager, vital for good decision making. Leadership expert and consultant Andrew Cox identified 10 important behaviors and thought habits necessary for being an effective and accurate observer:[7]

1   Sizing up people: people watching

2   Clarity: seeing the world as it is

3   Curiosity: asking why

4   Listening skills

5   Willingness to set aside personal biases

6   Willingness to seek the input of others

7   Seeking out new experiences and possibilities

8   Being comfortable with ambiguity

9   Knowledge of the behaviors and attitudes of people

10 Self-knowledge: accurately knowing your own behaviors, attitudes, and personal skills, and how they impact others

I like to refer to observation as "spectatorship." While being treated for cancer, I had a lot of time on my hands. Experiencing my own care was like watching a football game. This simile is easily applied to the healthcare setting (the playing field) and the management and staff in it (the coach and players). During a game one might notice a coach's body language and treatment of the players, the condition of the field, and the team's movement across the field as players perform together and individually.

Being in spectator mode during that time led to an epiphany for me: Successfully managing a PCE project requires an understanding of healing and a balance of process. (As discussed in Chapter 1, satisfying both requisites creates synergy in key areas of a project's life cycle so that even amid an ever-changing healthcare system, the scales will not be tipped so far toward project process that it overshadows the "human aspect" of healing.)

Having a spectator's vantage point greatly benefited me during one memorable project, a church renovation. The church board members who had hired me were accomplished business professionals, yet their individual agendas and strong egos were not always easy to manage. To familiarize myself with the physical space involved and better understand how the renovation might affect the parishioners, I attended a Sunday mass with my husband, paying close attention to what went on before and after the service.

As I watched the pastor move through the crowd and greet parishioners, I saw that he was well respected and could communicate with grace and style. I knew right then that I would rely primarily on him to support decisions and help me align the board members' thinking with the project's vision and scope, including the hiring of project team members. So, before I presented anything to them, I would hold a strategy session with the pastor, during which he and I could arrive at ideas for achieving consensus on important decisions.

For example, when it came time to choose a construction manager, I sent out bid-leveling documents to all the board members for their review a week before everyone was to meet and decide. By the morning of the meeting, each board member had an idea of which bid they wanted to go with from the three options on the table. But rather than have everyone reveal and then subsequently defend their choice of manager, I announced that we would hold a majority-rules vote on the matter and asked everyone to write down their vote and toss it into a passed hat. I counted the votes and announced the winner. This simple, tension-free process left everyone feeling heard because they could vote based on their own research and not have to debate others or even know whom their fellow board members had chosen.

My personal and direct interactions with the church leadership paid off tremendously in other ways, including during the construction phase and when working simultaneously with the board members and the project team. In this case, my background as a special-education teacher helped me hone my people instincts and observation skills. I find that, like younger students, some adults need to feel important, might have difficulty making decisions, or express frustration in unproductive ways. A good project manager will observe every member of the team and take note of unique assumptions, biases, agendas, and ways of interacting and coping. Stepping outside of one's own perceptions and into spectator mode can yield indispensable insights and sharpen decision making.

STOP, THINK, STRATEGIZE

Your field is fast-paced and chock-full of issues involving transparency, compliance, financial stress, risk, schedules, resources, and team dynamics. These concerns can be overwhelming enough. But add to them other distractions or the introduction of misinformation and your priorities can inadvertently shift away from fulfilling your project mission.

No doubt, leading a team can be stressful and involve great pressure, but at times you must remember to push aside the statistics and transactional tasks to remind yourself of what it is like to be a patient who has had a good or bad experience, a healthcare professional who is passionate about caring for patients, or another member of the project team. And why stop there? Take the time to tap into the needs and experiences of families, security personnel, facilities managers, and administrators, among others.

The strategy behind learning about stakeholders includes ensuring that they are heard—something that not all project leaders do. If you have not focused on this in the past, change your approach. Take a few minutes out of your hectic schedule to clear your head and focus on setting a general tone for leading the project that promotes harmony and supports everyone's activities.

MANAGE CLIENT IMPRESSIONS

It is not unusual in the healthcare industry to have team members themselves be clients, such as the director of facilities who officially hired you or the SVP of operations to whom you must provide monthly status reports. Having several clients on the same project can muddy up the waters. The one thing that you can be sure of is that all eyes will be on you. What message will you communicate to others about yourself? Executive image consultant Sylvie di Giusto stresses that it takes only 7 seconds for people to decide if you are a leader based on four factors: appearance, behavior, communication style, and digital footprint (how one presents themselves on the Internet).[8]

Managing your clients' perspectives begins with maximizing your professional appearance and communication style. Look good, act with confidence, and, above all, be authentic. Disseminate project information, such as budgets and schedules, clearly and concisely. Being able to break down complex ideas into digestible nuggets of knowledge can be one of your strongest attributes. Healthcare systems clients love it when their decision making is made easier, so make it easy for them to say, "Yes!" by being prepared, anticipating questions and objections, and by having alternative ideas or solutions at the ready.

RESPECT YOUR CREW

On the last day of a project, I received a call from the building engineer in charge of facilities, who told me that it had been a pleasure working with me and that he was sorry to see me go. He said that I was "good people," and that I knew what I was doing. As I hung up the phone after thanking him, I felt honored because here was a guy who I thought would never in a million years tell me how he felt about working with me. And then I thought about why he did it. I decided that it was because I had always been courteous to him and respectful of his time. At our meetings, I would look him in the eye, ask for his professional opinion, and let the team know that he was the overseer of the building systems, not me. After all, he would maintain the mechanical systems that we ultimately designed and installed.

Perhaps what made the greatest difference was that I made a sincere effort to connect with him on a personal level, including by asking questions about his family and what he did for pleasure. Cultivating a genuine curiosity about the people around you not only helps you to connect with them, it benefits you too. It is how we bond with others. We are compelled to seek common ground (in areas of career, family, sports, entertainment, politics, religion, hobbies, among others) in ways that foster tribal loyalty over time.

The point here is that although you can lead a team, you cannot control a team. You can only control yourself. However, if you act with integrity and respect each team member for who they are professionally and personally, the investment will come back to you in good ways. Your team members might be engineers, architects, or nurses, but they are first and foremost people who want to be treated with kindness, made to feel important, and be given a chance to share their wisdom and experience. Usually everyone comes to work wanting to do a good job and so they deserve the chance to rise to the occasion.

Building a Great Project Team

In his management book, *Good to Great: Why Some Companies Make the Leap ... And Others Don't,* Jim Collins emphasizes the mantra of "first who ... then what" as a key concept behind elevating a company. Rather than begin a project by setting a vision and determining a strategy, people who build great organizations "first get the right people on the bus, the wrong people off the bus, and the right people in the right seats—and then they figure out where to drive it."[9] Since one cannot possibly predict the future, the best management strategy is to have a team of people who can adapt to any situation and perform brilliantly even amid chaos and uncertainty.

You have to find the sweet spot, however. If you begin a project without the right team in place, you will not be able to leverage critical stakeholder wisdom and experience or build synergy among the members, which could have a negative impact on the quality of patient care delivered in a newly built PCE. Conversely, if you do have the right people on your team, but lack the communication and leadership skills to hear from everyone involved, you will waste valuable resources, including money.

COMPASSION, COLLABORATION, INNOVATION

One of the worst experiences for a design or construction professional is to have administrative or medical professionals begin working in a newly built environment only to subsequently ask, "What was the design team thinking? This will not serve our patients." Practicing compassionate, collaborative, innovative thinking during the planning, implementation, and construction phases of a project will prevent this outcome by keeping frustration levels low and the benefits of design efforts high.

Today's PCEs must reflect a "culture of health," broadly defined as an environment that supports good health and equity in healthcare decision making across all patient demographic groups. Building a suitable environment in which such a culture can thrive requires approaching a project with compassion and working within the existing parameters of the healthcare system to fully consider the needs of broad and diverse populations of patients and healthcare professionals. Ideally, team members would apply their instincts, expertise, and desire to achieve the project's mission.

Through collaboration, a team remains clear, focused, and efficient regarding what needs improvement and why. Innovation, meanwhile, is the outcome of the alignment and development of ideas. It is the point at which the "magic" happens and is only possible through research, strategic risk taking, and a willingness to fail and go back to the drawing board.

UNDERSTANDING STAKEHOLDER NEEDS

The challenges that a project manager faces when taking on a project involving different stakeholders can be daunting because knowledge levels will vary and not everyone will fully understand what is required of them as a team member. Also, "the more" might not always be "the merrier." Managing many people could feel a bit like herding cats. An *Inside Health* article from the Harvard T. H. Chan School of Public Health titled, "A Primer on Project Management for Health Care" states, "The number of stakeholders increases complexity. Similarly, healthcare project teams may be larger and more diverse due to the inherently cross-functional nature of patient care, requiring a project manager who is flexible and willing to take all views into consideration. Projects in healthcare may require more approvers or more buy-in; it's important that all parties be identified in the planning stage to avoid delays in the execution stage."[10]

As project leader, you can handle this situation by knowing each person's role—including the challenges that come with it—and by communicating both the general concepts and details of a project in layperson terms so that everyone is clear on the basics of building a PCE. This said, no project team can truly be effective without considering the perspectives and needs of all stakeholders inside and outside the organization. And since team members themselves are often stakeholders, no project manager can successfully lead a team unless he or she truly recognizes the diverse needs of a group of people who have come together, perhaps for the very first time, to achieve a common goal.

Becca Nell urges managers to take the tougher road when it comes to stakeholders by asking the necessary difficult questions, even if it means generating more work and dealing with bigger headaches. It is the only way to fully survey all stakeholder needs, assumptions, and expectations.

This is especially important when team members are healthcare professionals who have the added pressure of representing their peers (the users of the space being created). It is not enough to provide them with just the tangible necessities (office furniture, computer equipment, etc.). They are already tuned in to a *Healthy Patient* mindset and heavily invested in its principles. To truly empower these people in their new environment, the *Healthy Team* as a whole must value their fellow team members' experiences and go beyond the practical considerations of space usage, personnel interactions, and formal protocols of patient care.

For example, I once worked on a long-overdue, major overhaul of a medical surgical wing. We had a limited budget but were nevertheless expected to balance the costs of the extensive improvements that had to be made with the costs of fulfilling the needs and priorities of the medical team, support staff (IT and telecom personnel, medical equipment vendors), and patients. Fortunately, we had a great project team that included members from the medical surgery unit who were proactive in soliciting valuable input and perspectives from the nurses who worked in the wing. For example, the nurses recounted stories about patients who were recovering from orthopedic procedures being unable to use the restroom independently because its doorway was not wide enough to accommodate the use of walkers. Patients had to call for an aide and use a bedpan, which caused them undue embarrassment, took them longer to heal (according to the nurses), and created more work for the staff.

This was unacceptable to the team, which was committed to a patient care philosophy of helping patients recover faster and maintain their sense of dignity, while reducing the workload for nurses and aides, and so our renovation plans included widening the bathroom door. By also reducing the size of the patient room closet and purchasing a new bed table for the smaller space, we wound up solving a long-standing quality-of-care issue. All it took was listening to our stakeholders and respecting their points of view.

The willingness to drill down into a project beyond blueprints and Gantt charts acknowledges the duality of the healthcare professional, who is at once scientifically minded and deeply passionate about his or her work. What bridges the mind and heart is the spirit, which allows dedicated individuals to build relationships with patients that center on providing comfort, compassion, and empathy. Establishing a connection enhances patient engagement, which can aid in the diagnostic process and determining the best treatment plan. It is also vitally important to healthcare professionals because the "product" they are concerned with is not providing healthcare per se, but providing "caring." Being mindful of this priority when observing and listening to team members will positively inform the design of novel and effective PCEs.

Of course, healthcare professionals are not the only project stakeholders with needs. When we built the Cohen Children's Specialty Center in Stamford, Connecticut, we set out to bring highly skilled pediatric specialists into the community to address the unique needs of young patients. We had the good fortune of working with the Steven & Alexandra Cohen Foundation to define the project priorities and parameters from the outset. The Cohens are known for their dedication to improving children's health, and the foundation's involvement gave our center more exposure and the creative freedom to design a bit out of the box. To respect and cultivate this important relationship, we communicated with the foundation's representative in a way that kept funders fully informed, including regarding how short-term changes would affect the outcome of the funding strategy in the long term.

Whether you deal with donors, vendors, or consultants, the likelihood of problems arising during the project will be lessened if you first define your working relationships. When your stakeholders feel that their opinions and needs matter to the project team, you will enjoy broader cooperation and be better able to build trusting relationships. Establishing strong stakeholder connections is not always easy. I have even seen team members whom I would describe as "project management abused," meaning that they have not always felt valued as partners, both in the services that they provide and in their compensation.

An example of this that I see frequently is when I ask outside consultants to perform a task and they hesitate to raise any issues or even complete the work. I would later discover that they were not being properly compensated, a completely unacceptable situation, since negotiating fees and contracts involves ensuring that a consultant's work be valued. It not only makes outside professionals become more invested as team members, it helps build trust among everyone, preserve the schedule, and save money in the long run.

MOTIVATIONS, VALUES, AND EXPECTATIONS

Underlying the success of any project is being clear on people's individual motivations, values, and expectations, and then meeting them where they are. Rather than expect to have everyone assimilate into the project in a homogenous way, which can compromise buy-in and undercut engagement, it is better to find out what drives each team member and make the most of that information so that it benefits you as a manager, respects the team member, and supports the project.

To leverage the individual strengths of your team and guide everyone to success, do some up-front sleuthing about motivations, values, and expectations. Find out why people are on the team, make sure that everyone belongs on the team, and be confident that everyone has internalized the same goals.

What Is in It for Everyone?

Members on a project team should be motivated by the knowledge that what they do for a living matters and that the quality of patient care delivered in a PCE relies in part on their successful project participation. Help your team accept the fact that how a patient heals will in turn affect that person's everyday life. Simply put, efforts to create a PCE will be significantly enhanced if your team finds the work to be personally meaningful.

Fortunately, you will encounter stakeholders who are already very motivated. If you ask a healthcare worker why they chose their field, you might hear a story about how she or he, or a family member, was ill and how a nurse or clinician made an impression strong enough to compel that team member to pay it forward. But personal reasons aside, there are practical motivations for inspiring a team to commit to a project well done. In addition to benefiting individual careers, a well-executed PCE serves as a powerful defining symbol that broadcasts an institution's "brand" to its community.

Prior to project kickoff, the team should know the answers to basic questions regarding the healthcare system's motivations:

1   Why are we building this environment? (Have your team identify and connect to the "why" of the project from the start.)

2   Is this project part of the healthcare system's master plan or a one-off assignment?

3   What patient care model or patient-centric philosophy will we use to guide us and keep us focused on a *Healthy Patient* approach?

4   What is the C-suite's leadership style and levels of
    commitment, support, and follow-through capability?
    Have top-level decision makers approved the project?

5   What is the intended impact of the final design and
    functionality of the new PCE on the health and wellness
    of the patients and staff?

The Patient Advisory Board

A few years ago, I was asked to serve on a patient advisory board
(PAB). As I witnessed the politics, passion, and dedication displayed
by the board members in addressing the issues and challenges
of the healthcare system, I concluded that we were walking a
tightrope between what the PAB believed should be improved
versus what the hospital administration could allow based on
compliance issues and cost concerns.

As patients of the hospital and members of the broader
community, the PAB members applied their patient care
experiences—good and bad—to the mission of advising on needed
healthcare system improvements, which included a new billing
system, a revamped hospital discharge process, a patient rights
and policies manual, pre-surgery training and communications,
the design and construction of a new patient bed tower, and
better wayfinding.

Many of the PAB's proposed solutions, although good, were cost
prohibitive. Unfortunately, cost is often a touchy subject, and a
lack of knowledge on the part of patient advisors can sometimes
complicate your efforts to be politically correct and to maintain
a stress-free atmosphere between two well-intentioned groups.

For example, a board member might suggest a contractor who he or she thinks can complete a project better and cheaper without having considered important cost factors.

To avoid stoking any tensions and to foster productivity, I always took the initiative of stepping into a teaching role. I would ascertain how much the members knew about the facts and realities behind the project, and then make sure to present costs and estimates clearly and up front. I worked to establish a collaborative atmosphere for problem solving by listening and acknowledging the board's perspectives and by demonstrating a willingness to find solutions. I always kept in mind that the board was made up of individuals who were selflessly donating their time and doing it for the good of the community. I did not want to inadvertently discourage this attitude.

When you find yourself in a similar situation, remember that no single idea is necessarily the only "right" idea. I rely on the sage advice that my friend Phil. M. Jones provides in his book, *Exactly What to Say: The Magic Words for Influence and Impact,* and tell the PAB, "In my experience what most people do is ...." According to Phil, by taking an indirect "safety in numbers" approach, you can prompt people to do what is needed without actually telling them. But make sure to set parameters for everyone's roles early on, so that the PAB understands its advisory role and that the hospital administration will have the final say.

In addition to working with PABs, you will interact with outside consultants who enjoy what they do for a living and actively participate in their communities. Understandably, they want to preserve their reputations to be considered for subsequent projects. Whatever the motivations of your stakeholders, it is your job as the project manager to make them feel heard and empowered by learning the "why" behind their involvement on the team. Once you know their intentions, you can build harmonious working relationships.

Is the Team a Good Fit?

A project manager's job is to make sure that team members are a good fit for a given project, for the sake of the people and the success of the project. I was once brought into a project in deep trouble. Going into spectator mode, I noticed that the team was operating in a very dysfunctional way. Two camps were at odds: a contractor who had overpromised and underdelivered and an owner with unrealistic expectations. Team interactions were disrespectful and unproductive. For example, at weekly meetings, certain team members ordered the rest of the team not to talk and declared that they would be the ones asking the questions. This made no sense because we all had important contributions to make. After being shut down, we decided it was best to not say anything, which meant that many important concerns were kept from the owner.

Month after month, the owner refused to give up her unrealistic expectations, and so the behaviors further fueled the problems. Finally, after the owner wound up paying for several consultants to come in and fix the problems, she listened to our advice and fired the contractor to get the project back on track. It all came down to the owner's values, which were self-serving and centered on a budget and schedule that she thought would save money by sticking with the existing contractor. Instead, it cost her much more in the long run because the contractor prevented the team from meeting project milestones, the consultants were pulled down because of it, and the quality of the project suffered from all the mistakes and change orders.

At the end of the day, the main problem was that the owner did not trust the people on the team. Projects are not about planning and executing tasks in a vacuum, but rather about accounting for different value systems. Projects succeed when teamwork is valued—when everyone places the same importance on a shared goal and is willing to support each other to achieve it. Team members who value a project have the integrity, trustworthiness, and commitment to maintaining the high standards necessary to make the project a success.

Therefore, project leaders must not only listen to the words being spoken, but also recognize the intent behind them to gauge what team members are really trying to communicate and to identify their value systems. Unfortunately, the team members mentioned earlier who were alienating others on the project were more concerned with what they had to say than with considering the opinions or concerns of others. The proof was in the pudding with less-than-stellar project results. Although the contractor was dismissed and a new team was hired to finish the project, the lack of trust and effective communication persistently manifested in subsequent quality-of-work issues.

Are We on the Same Page?

In the previous story, you might have wondered why the owner clung steadfastly to her unrealistic expectations. Had the consultants not spoken up about the details of the budget or schedule, or did the owner simply refuse to listen? Was information being withheld among the team ranks? Was the owner so overloaded with work that she could not keep track of project details? Did she assume that since the project was based in New York City that any conceivable idea could be realized?

Regardless of the reasons behind this project failure, emerging issues should have been identified and nipped in the bud. One way to do this is by transforming information into digestible nuggets to explain why expectations are not on track and to disseminate that information in a timely way. Ask probing questions that help people understand why their expectations might not align with reality. No matter how frustrating it might be, keep asking until a light bulb goes off in people's heads. For example:

1   What are the vision and mission of the organization?

2   What is the organization's culture?

3   Who is the patient whom we are serving?

4   What is the project scope?

5   Do the budget and schedule make sense?

6   Do you feel that I as project manager am clear on your expectations?

7   Do I have the right team?

LEVERAGING WISDOM AND EXPERIENCE

Have you ever been privy to inside information that you would not have otherwise known but which helped you avoid a disaster—like knowing that the president of the organization does not like the color-coding system used for wayfinding in parking garages? Team members possess valuable institutional knowledge and familiarity with their organization's culture. In pursuing the same goal, a *Healthy Team* can share its collective wisdom and experience to meet patient and staff needs and facilitate getting a patient from illness to wellness. Members with extensive career experience and hard-won insights can quickly identify, contain, and resolve problems, which is critical on so many fronts when designing and building a PCE.

As project leader, you must encourage unity and nurture a collaborative spirit, ideally by modeling it yourself every day. Make participants feel that what they say matters and convince them to share their thoughts and insights regarding every aspect of project's life cycle, from design specifications to infection prevention to safety and logistics.

NUTS AND BOLTS

There are many ways to get your project off to a good start, but no better one than to get everyone together in a room or on a teleconference call to make introductions, run through each person's role, and convey the time commitment required for the project.

Having everyone on the same page from the get-go means less chance for subsequent miscommunication and misunderstanding and a greater likelihood of cooperation and accountability.

As you plan your first meeting, consider it as being not that much different from throwing a great party. You need a good reason to have a party, and then you have to pick the right date, time, and setting, put together the best invitation list, set up the right supporting "technology," and have refreshments available.

Sounds simple, right? It can be if you take the right steps. Otherwise, you might give the team the wrong idea or be perceived as a time waster or someone who lacks strong leadership skills. Early on, you need to earn your team's respect regarding your ability to organize a purposeful meeting and spend their time efficiently.

 HELPFUL TIPS

Here is a list of important steps to take to ensure that your project launch goes off without a hitch and leaves your new team feeling excited and ready to take on any challenge:

[1]   **Send out invitations to potential team members.** In your meeting invitation explain the project vision and the importance of the invitee's participation.

[2]   **Send out the first meeting agenda well in advance.** Be clear on the purpose and details of the meeting, including how it will take place, how long it will run, and what to bring, if anything.

[3]   **Create a comfortable setting.** Reserve a climate-controlled meeting room that can accommodate the group. You will need adequate and comfortable seating, proper lighting, and working technology for sharing information with everyone, including participants who are off-site.

[4]   **Provide refreshments.** If it is an early morning meeting, serve breakfast. It might be an added cost, but you will be addressing an alert team. Accommodating special dietary needs can be a thoughtful touch.

[5]   **Welcome everyone.** As they enter the meeting room, greet attendees as you would welcome a visitor to your home. Ask each person a probing question, something personal but fun: "What was the first car you owned?" Engaging people in something off-topic can yield insights into their personalities and encourage them to share information about themselves, which could help them open up later.

[6]   **Stick to the meeting structure.** Begin the meeting on time, introduce yourself, and review agenda points and meeting goals.

[7] **Wrap up the meeting efficiently.** At the end of the meeting, remind everyone of the important points of the meeting and of each attendee's tasks and deadlines. Then determine a time for the team to meet on a regular basis. (Ideally, you should meet at the same time and place each week, since an established routine is hard to break.)

[8] **Thank everyone.** As they leave the meeting, thank attendees individually for their time and input.

[9] **Send out a meeting summary.** As soon as you can, follow up the meeting with a documented recap of key points and to-dos.

(Additional information on instituting process and controls can be found in Chapter 3, page 141.)

Welcome Professional Diversity

There are as many different types of *Healthy Teams* as there are projects. Your institution's "authority having jurisdiction" (AHJ) will require that an interdisciplinary team of professionals be in place to comply with government rules and requirements (such as state certificates of need), board member approval, and hospital funding, among other project concerns. (*See* Resources, page 294.)

Unfortunately, many projects are run without the participation of individuals who will be affected by the newly built environment. An old-school fear is that if too many people are involved nothing will get done, when the opposite is true. When you have everyone's input, you are less likely to miss important details.

But this depends on your cultivating a culture of trust in the team, facilitating good communication and collaboration, and maintaining accountability so that every person's point of view can be considered.

FIRST IMPRESSIONS

A good project manager will welcome people from different disciplines, experiences, and perspectives and bring them together to accomplish a shared goal. At times you will not have the luxury of choosing your own team, such as when you are a latecomer to a project, in which case you must exercise good management skills by learning about each team member.

This should not be terribly difficult given social media and the power of Google. That said, remember that while getting a quick take on someone might be easy, online snapshots might not give you an accurate impression of a person, especially since personas are often shaped to serve self-marketing purposes. Nothing can substitute for firsthand observations of a person interacting with you and others. Remain in full spectator mode until you know how you will likely be working with each team member.

A personal example that I use to describe bringing together a diverse group of people is the opening of my ski house. First, I must find folks who love to ski or who are at least curious enough to learn. I then send out invitations, prepare the house for a warm, comfortable welcome, finalize sleeping arrangements, determine food assignments, and provide my guests with instructions, travel tips, gear lists, and other resources. After throwing in some rules for wearing helmets, keeping walkways clear, and managing rooms and sharing the bathroom, we are good to go. I have done all I can to make my guests—each of whom has a different viewpoint and skill level—feel comfortable and ready for a shared experience.

This is not far afield from how I respect the diversity of my project teams. My management method involves mentally dividing team members into two groups: the medical experts and the construction professionals. I then gauge the experience and knowledge levels of each group and customize how I present project information. For example, I have worked on projects where physicians wanted to be involved in the demolition phase. Their construction experience might have stemmed from a home renovation or they might simply love demolition in general. Understanding the basis for their project participation and levels of enthusiasm was extremely valuable. A team member's lack of enthusiasm for a PCE project or even mistrust of the construction professionals involved could stem from a terrible home renovation experience.

Conversely, construction professionals on a project might not know the technical and patient-related considerations behind the medical procedures to be performed in a new space. You have to figure out what they do not know, as well as be familiar with the tasks or methodologies they plan to use. For example, I will ask a construction manager about the level of noise or vibration that a construction task might create for patients and staff, which could be significant. No detail is too big or small. Even something as simple as asking end users to properly label their moving boxes can avoid a logistical headache of epic proportions. Thinking ahead stems from a willingness to understand how professionals think and operate.

QUESTIONS TO ASK

Because there is diversity in culture, religion, skill level, age, and professional specialties and backgrounds, you must always ask questions, a habit that I cannot emphasize enough. Posing simple questions creates openings for people to explain their feelings, beliefs, or understanding.

What follows are sample questions to ask your team members during the early stages of a project. The conversations that result from asking these questions will help build working relationships and crystalize the group's intentions.

- How open-minded are you? Who in this room thinks that they are open-minded?

- How can we involve staff in strategy, operations, and planning for the future?

- How will the definition of "care" influence what we build?

- What can competitors in our area teach us?

Cultivate Collaboration

Establishing a collaborative, interactive atmosphere should be a priority during initial team-building efforts. Collaboration is an art that must be practiced every day by both manager and team member because it does not necessarily occur naturally. You must often plan ways in which your team members can interact among themselves and with you. The effort will go far in making everyone feel comfortable about sharing their personal wisdom and experience.

 ## EXERCISE 1

To foster a collaborative atmosphere, kick off things with a light-hearted, yet productive "business improv" exercise, in which a team of performers "plays" together to achieve a goal. It will require clear communication, the giving and taking of control, and a willingness to make each other look good. (It is no coincidence that these are qualities fundamental to the success of any business team.)

Avish Parashar is a successful motivational improviser who teaches business improv exercises to help teams, departments, and organizations improve creativity, decrease stress, hone leadership skills, and be open to change, among other benefits.[11] He especially recommends the "two-word story."

Break up your team into pairs and ask them to create a story by having each partner think up only two words of the story at a time. For example, one person opens with, "One day," the second persons adds, "there was," the first person says, "a dog," and so on. The resulting tale will be funny and unusual, even wacky. To maximize creativity, remind participants not to overthink anything and to just keep the story moving quickly, even if someone accidentally offers up more than two words.

EXERCISE 2

Another way to cultivate a collaborative atmosphere is to learn more about the culture of the healthcare system you are serving, as well as determining the level of your team's compassion, uncovering their values, and reinforcing the project's strategic mission. This can be creatively accomplished by having team members work together in "unlikely" teams.

Pair off a nurse and an engineer and ask them to consider a project-specific question, such as, "What is the best location for a hand-washing sink in the hallway?" or "How can we fit this monitor into such a small space?" Then have them present their answer to the group. Pairing two types of professionals sharpens their individual problem-solving skills by forcing them to consider a problem from a different value or needs perspective, by staying focused on a goal, and by understanding what is or is not possible and why.

 QUESTIONS TO ASK

There are additional ways to motivate people to come together on a shared mission and to adopt a group philosophy:

[1] **Ask healthcare professionals on the team if they follow an institutional patient care philosophy.** For example, the mission of Planetree, a pioneer in patient-centered care, includes a patient care philosophy that recognizes nine core components and is strongly committed to establishing and

maintaining a specific organizational culture. Since patient care philosophies vary across healthcare systems, reviewing this information will help orient and focus team members on the specifics, which will make your life easier.

[2] **Find out if the institution works with a patient and family advisory council (PFAC).** If so, ask whether it is involved in decision making on institutional projects. If it has active participants whose voices are honored, pick a member to serve as a liaison who can help you determine the best time to present plans to the PFAC or provide valuable feedback during an environment prototype walkthrough.

[3] **Know the source of project funding.** This includes knowing how to direct expenses to the right cost centers. Every detail matters. Are there special funds dedicated to a portion of purchased equipment? Are there donor requests to honor? Involve the team to remind them of the need to administer funds correctly. For example, if the emergency department has a grant to buy equipment for EMTs, then the money can only be used for that purpose.

Build Connections

Successful project management means paying attention to the power of human connectivity, kindness, and preparedness. A welcoming, well-prepared environment sets the stage for productive and satisfying interactions and the cultivation of camaraderie. During my initial project meetings, I will look around the room at everyone to determine how I might establish a team culture that will nurture the potential in everyone and build raw talents into strengths. I develop a "people plan," much as a teacher might build a lesson plan based on a student's current knowledge base, learning style, confidence level, and basic need for good self-esteem.

EXERCISE 3

Think about the people recruited to be on your team. What do they value, what excites them, what are their thinking styles? How successfully do you see them interacting with others?

For example, creative thinkers and linear thinkers can benefit tremendously from each other's input—or they can drive each other crazy. Still, collaboration can yield new insights and approaches to doing things, benefiting both individuals and the healthcare system. Your task is to balance different groups synergistically, so that team members can arrive at strong, achievable ideas.

Pair a new hire with a seasoned professional and give them a problem to solve. For example, ask a young engineer and an experienced electrical supervisor to find a way to update electronic files for electrical equipment. The junior engineer might well have a technology solution unknown to the experienced engineer.

QUESTIONS TO ASK

Establishing a sense of belonging among team members begins with inspiring confidence. As the leader, you can shine a light on each member's importance to the success of the team by gauging baseline attitudes. Have a team conversation and take detailed notes. Observe closely, ask questions, and conduct one-on-one interviews. Ask yourself the following questions early on to guide your efforts:

- How confident are the team members in their knowledge of building a patient-centered healthcare environment?

- Do they feel that PCEs are indispensable or overrated?

- Do they appear genuinely committed to the project goals?

- Are team members assessing the functionality of the space not from just their own perspective, but also through the eyes of patients and family members?

- Is the team comfortable with talking about the personal and emotional aspects associated with PCEs?

The answers to these and related questions can help you determine if everyone is on board. If some members appear less than fully committed, help them establish a sense of purpose by talking to them about how it can benefit them personally. Encourage compassion. Thupten Jinpa, scholar, author of *A Fearless Heart*, and the Dalai Lama's decades-long principal

English translator, reminds us that, "When we help someone with genuine concern ... levels of endorphins, which are associated with euphoric feeling, surge in the brain, a phenomenon referred to as the 'helper's high.'"[12] Help team members understand that by investing themselves in the project they can make a difference in someone's life, which should make them feel good.

EXERCISE 4

Fortunately, most healthcare professionals already demonstrate great compassion, although it never hurts to reinforce the trait by assigning an exercise that can also reaffirm one's sense of purpose and connection to a common goal. Participants begin by recounting a stressful experience first from their own perspective, followed by the perspective of a loved one, and then of a stranger.

[1] Begin by asking team members to tell you what they would do if they were just diagnosed with a rare disease. How would they feel? Where would they go to think about what just happened?

[2] Next, ask them to recount a story about a family member's healthcare experience, good or bad. How did it make the loved one feel? Were team members able to help them with their experience? What would they have changed if they could?

[3] Finally, ask team members to imagine a stranger being admitted to the hospital without a support person. How would the person feel and what would his or her worry be regarding being alone at such a vulnerable time?

These questions prompt your team to exercise their compassion and collaborative communication skills by putting themselves in the shoes of someone dealing with a healthcare event, which can inform the design of an environment so that it reflects the qualities of sympathy, empathy, compassion, and open-mindedness.

Establish Roles and Responsibilities

Once you have identified your team members and have a good sense of their motivations and expectations you can establish discrete roles and delegate responsibilities. Unfortunately, you might sometimes not have the opportunity to observe individual personalities and interaction styles. Although a lack of such information might hamper the situation, you need to move ahead regardless and revise assignments later if necessary.

 HELPFUL TIPS

Team members have more trust in project managers who clearly communicate what team participation entails and who actively listen to the team's observations and concerns. This is an ongoing process, since new team members can be recruited throughout the initiation and planning phases of a project (*see* Chapter 3, "Healthy Project").

The sooner you identify needs, the more informed and proactive you will be in keeping everyone on track and focused, and thereby more productive throughout the project.

Some additional advice:

[1]   **Do not skip formal introductions**. At the kickoff meeting, make sure everyone knows who everyone is, what department or company they work in, and their roles: "This is Brenda, the infection prevention nurse. Her role will be to assist the team in designing an infection-free, safe environment. She will help us with sink locations, hand sanitizer dispensers, glove boxes, soap dispensers, and needle boxes, and she will also sign off on our ICRA paperwork." Detailed information helps the team iron out the staff workflow processes that will be built into the environment.

[2]   **Clarify your managerial role.** Whether done privately or in front of the group, let participants know about your own thinking and interaction styles, as well as your expectations as the project manager. This will allow for better team communication and engagement.

[3]   **Leave no team member behind.** If anyone exhibits a deer-in-the-headlights look about their assigned role and responsibilities, pull them aside after the meeting and clear up any confusion.

Match Skills to Tasks

Having taught in the classroom before stepping into the corporate world has been of indispensable value to me because I can apply my specialized training to the world of project management. When working with students, you need to keep them inspired and motivated for learning. You must understand their behavior, help them focus, and identify the classroom leaders. Back then I often used peer pressure to maintain order by leaning on the leaders for their advice and assistance in persuading the rest of the group to stay on track with the day's lessons. I also relied on standardized tests to gauge reading aptitude and decision-making ability. Armed with the results, I tailored learning programs to individual learning styles and abilities.

It would be nice if in the working world we could determine in advance how well team members might work together. However, project managers generally do not have access to such information when they take on a project team. And even if personality trait data were made available through such tools as the Myers-Briggs Type Indicator or Gallup's StrengthsFinder 2.0, the jury is still out on the value of the data in shaping team dynamics.

So how can you uncover the personalities, expertise, and behaviors of your team members? You might initially think that it is not your job to take stock of different personalities. Do you really need to take on that work? Yes, you do and should. Think of the advantages for project management—and the potential benefits to the team itself—if you could understand each member's personality and its potential impact on teamwork. You could match a person's skills to the right tasks, communicate more effectively, keep the peace, leverage strengths and mitigate weaknesses, and foster the team harmony needed to focus on "strategy execution."

In his *Harvard Business Review* article, Peter Bregman writes, "Execution is a people problem not a strategy problem," and he points out the large gap between what a person knows and what he or she does. Strategy development and communication are about "knowing" something, while strategy execution is about "doing" something. To get something done with your team, you need to assess everyone's technical expertise, working style, and level of understanding of design and construction process. When working with medical professionals who are not familiar with building PCEs, you need to make them feel comfortable instead of intimidated.

BUSINESS PERSONALITIES

While writing this book, I researched several personality tests that covered work styles and how they affect teams. One system that is straightforward enough to use out of the box is "Business Chemistry," developed by Deloitte. It relies on science-based analytics to identify four primary business style behaviors and offers related strategies for accomplishing shared goals. Each behavioral group presents useful real-world perspectives and distinctive approaches to ideation, decision making, and problem solving.

Pioneers

Pioneers are people who bring the world of possibility to a project by sparking imagination and contributing a can-do level of energy to the team. Pioneers are spontaneous and adaptable. They believe that risks are worth taking and that it is important to go with one's gut. Pioneers focus on the big picture and are drawn to bold new ideas and creative approaches. Ideally, you should have pioneers on your team, especially during the initiation phase of a project, given how they can fuel innovative thinking and brainstorming. But know that pioneers do not always appreciate it when another group, guardians, calls for facts to back up their ideas.

Guardians

Because stability and practicality are what guardians value, these individuals tend to bring order and rigor to a project. Guardians hesitate to embrace risk due to their pragmatic nature. For them, data and facts are baseline requirements and details matter. Guardians think it makes sense to learn from the past. They relish structure and are the ones who usually introduce evidence and facts into a project (they are oftentimes engineers or architects). In the healthcare industry, guardians expect ideas to be backed by evidence. Pioneers might rattle their cages, so you need to smartly manage how these two types of people work together.

Drivers

Drivers operate from a quantitative, technical perspective and value a challenge. They can generate momentum in a team because they are oriented toward getting results and winning. To them a project is a black-and-white affair, and they will tackle problems head on, armed with logic and data. Drivers are competitive and will keep things rolling, even when the going gets tough, but they can also be blunt in their communications, so you should help them channel their energy productively.

Integrators

Relationships and a sense of responsibility to the group are paramount for these empathetic individuals, who value connection, draw teams together, and tend to believe that most circumstances are relative. Integrators want everyone to get along and play nicely in the sandbox. They use their talents in diplomacy and consensus building to achieve harmony, yet might get upset if pioneers and drivers on the team are not aligned with their thinking. To keep a project moving forward, you might rely on integrators to keep everyone working well together and on the same page.

 ## HELPFUL TIPS

When I learned about behavior archetypes, a light bulb went off for me. Although we naturally tend to gravitate toward people who share our own work style, it is worthwhile to step out of our comfort zone to experience the benefits of personality diversity in the workplace.

By understanding even basic team dynamics, you can tailor your presentations—including modifying your language when responding to questions—to make people with other behavior styles more receptive to your messaging. A few tips:

[1]   **Write it down.** Keep a team journal and record what you know or have observed about your team members. It will keep you from forgetting or mixing up details about a person, even something as simple as a name. You also never know how a fact or story recounted by a team member could prove useful at a later point.

[2]   **Have a game plan in place.** Leverage what you know about your team to delegate the right tasks to the right people. Test your theories and refine your plan to give everyone on the team the opportunity to shine.

[3] **Study your team.** Know the answers to the following questions about your team members:

- What personality strengths do you see in each member? Are they compassionate, innovative, collaborative, etc.?

- What are his or her core personal values? What is their family life like? What do they enjoy outside of work?

- What expertise or skills do they bring to the project, and does this experience include having been on PCE project teams?

- Do team members understand the basic principles of design and construction?

- What is each member's business style based on the Business Chemistry system? (This might take a while to determine, so pay attention and note that people can be a mix of more than one type.)

- What are the assigned responsibilities of healthcare system employees? How do external team members fit in? To whom do these participants report if not to you?

- Who on the team can work independently?

- How much time can each person dedicate to the project? Who will be approving everyone's contracts and invoices?

Mine for Input

Can you obligate someone to share information? Possibly. But making them feel important and supported are better ways to gain information and build trust, a task that requires communicating effectively and recognizing that people approach their work in different ways. Individuals can be extroverts or introverts, on the cautious side or entirely trusting. And even if you can get a general read on someone, their experiences and wisdom might not be immediately evident. In fact, I often find that quieter team members can have some of the best insights, but getting their input might not be easy. They might be "guardians" with valuable information.

Nevertheless, you must find a way because specialists add cultural and intellectual diversity to the team. But be sensitive to anyone who might feel out of their comfort zone. A creative approach and a sense of humor can go a long way in keeping people talking and revealing the answers that you seek.

Many years ago, I had two engineers on my team who didn't speak during meetings. They were guardians. One day I referred to them as my experts and asked them to share their ideas on an issue. They suddenly let loose a torrent of relevant, problem-solving information. Why? Because they saw that I did not have all the answers. I also recognized that they had researched the existing building systems and knew how things worked together. All I had to do was ask.

How often do you ask your team members questions specific to their backgrounds? Do you seek out their expertise or do you make assumptions? There are plenty of project managers who will not even let their teams view physical plans, which can inhibit group participation, collaboration, and creative problem solving.

HELPFUL TIPS

Here are additional ways to elicit participation and input from your team (*see* Chapter 4, "The Art of Storytelling"):

[1] **Present hypothetical situations.** Some people withhold information for fear of having to commit to something or give a "wrong" answer. Seek their input by setting up a hypothetical situation that encourages them to speak freely. For example, I use the word "pretend" in my what-if scenarios: "Pretend that we are on schedule. How long might such-and-such take to finish?"

[2] **Gently guide the discussion.** When you ask a question and someone gives an irrelevant answer, either rephrase the question or simply say, "Great idea! We might be able to apply it to another situation." The positive response assures them that you are listening and that you welcome team participation.

[3] **Inject levity into a situation.** Tell a funny story about a struggle that you underwent related to the topic at hand. Humor breaks the ice for many people who might otherwise not open up.

[4] **Supplement with visuals.** Always have a set of plans or other relevant documents displayed during your meeting to support clearer communication and information sharing.

Deal with Wrench-Throwers

In the 1980s, I taught seventh-graders with learning disabilities. In the beginning, a few students tested me by coming late to class or acting out. Fortunately, I had a supportive department director who told me to keep good records and let the students know it. Each time something occurred, I would record the details. This made parent meetings more productive because students knew there existed a "book of facts." The result was a more peaceful and productive teaching environment for everyone.

Similarly, in the adult professional world, no matter how successful you are in the initial phases of team building, there will be people who challenge your management ideas. This is not to say that the negative response is intentional. Some people are unaware that they might be undermining a project's process. But to keep things moving you need to recognize and counter their strategies.

If someone's expectations are not aligned with yours or those of the team and might cause problems, try my aforementioned teaching strategy. Identify and document any "mismatches" to hold people accountable and maintain control of the project. Here are some examples of wrench-throwers whom you might encounter:

THE MEETING HATER

Although most of us do not relish meetings, many healthcare workers are particularly averse to them, preferring to care for their patients rather than sit in a conference room. For them, a meeting is just one more obligation added to an already overpacked schedule. It could be anyone with a lot on their plate—whether a surgeon, an ICU nurse, or an IT specialist. These individuals might ask to join a discussion via teleconference or a "go-to" meeting session. Unfortunately, many hospital conference rooms lack such capabilities, leaving it to the leader to come up with another idea.

In such a scenario, I might ask people for a "drive-by." Attendees would walk into an ongoing meeting, tell us how much time they had, and we would address their topics first. I would then officially throw them out of the meeting. (Once other team members saw this action they would beg that they, too, be officially thrown out of the meeting.)

You can also encourage meeting attendance by showing invitees that their participation is important. For example, we needed to temporarily relocate a 24/7 hospital pharmacy department without disrupting its operations. We invited a different pharmacist to each of our Monday morning meetings to solicit their input. In this case, it was the pharmacists, not IT personnel, who ruled our world. But they did not feel it was necessary to attend. I had to convince them that their wisdom and experience was valued by the team, especially by the architects and engineers who oversaw space planning and logistics. The pharmacists ultimately agreed, stepping out of their comfort zones to attend (helped in no small way by the lure of coffee and bagels). Your creativity as a leader will often come into play in such simple ways to maximize team participation.

THE CHAOS LOVER

Some people create chaos to make themselves feel important, but you can stop this undesirable behavior by convincing these team members that their opinions and participation *are* important. I once ran a project for a client whose CFO was never satisfied with the budget and schedule. He tried to negotiate pricing at every meeting, which stressed me out and made me dread the next meeting. I eventually stopped reacting to him, although I should have pegged him sooner as a person who would introduce conflict just for the sake of it.

Playing mind games makes some people feel powerful, but if you are wise to the tactic, you can plan ahead even if you have limited control. Although it might seem a counterintuitive approach, try involving these individuals more deeply in the project and keep them informed with plenty of straightforward information. The CFO I dealt with was a numbers guy, so I kept him at bay with an information-rich spreadsheet.

Above all, stay calm and do not let chaos lovers rattle you, try as they might. Keep to the facts and wait things out if necessary.

THE C-SUITE TABLE-TURNER

Back in 2003, I struggled with persuading the directors of an IT department to follow my project management approach to build a hospital computer room. Their reticence was likely due to their inexperience with the construction project process and its intricacies. After a few weeks and some meetings, I finally got them on board, but there was another hurdle to clear. The VP to whom both directors reported—"Teflon Man" as I called him—expected the project to be completed despite a woefully underfunded budget. After ordering me to begin the project, I answered, "I can start the project if you sign off on the proposal for the contractor and add additional money to the budget." He ignored my request, assuming that I would move forward with the work anyway.

After a few heated conversations that went nowhere, I finally spoke to my boss, who asked me to put together a presentation on the history of the project and the cost variance concerns we had. We arranged a meeting with the VP and the CFO. With my boss's executive-level support, I could make my case using facts to show that if the hospital wanted the project completed, they would have to increase the budget. The CFO was receptive because the data was there for him in black and white. As for Teflon Man, he remained an obstacle to the end, but he became less of a concern.

To work around obstructers, you need to understand the political landscape and be willing to reach out for help. As much as I would have loved to have simply explained my situation to the CFO, I had to go through my supervisor to get what I needed. Uncooperative behavior and a lack of support should not dissuade you from seeking out the right person who can break an executive-level logjam. Remain agile and determined.

THE INFORMATION BOTTLENECKER

You know the phrase "information is power." Well, information bottleneckers live by these words. Keeping information close to the vest makes them feel important, but this action can sabotage your project and must be controlled.

The first step in dealing with information bottlenecking is to confirm which individual (or group) is withholding information. Ask appropriate questions and note behavior patterns. If you learn that the act was unintentional, give the person the benefit of the doubt, but keep an eye out in case information is again withheld and you need to change up your strategy.

It will also help to uncover the motivations for this behavior, such as a possible disconnection or alienation from the team. Every situation is different with unique solutions, but keep in mind that the withholding of information can be toxic for the team. In extreme cases, you could consider asking the person to leave the team if you have the authority. If not, enlist your team's help to get what you need on a timely basis.

Never Forgo "People Care"

Understanding people, making connections, and cultivating an atmosphere of belonging are the central components of what I call a "people care plan." On any PCE project, you will need a strategy for dealing with "people stuff," since managing, motivating, and letting your people learn by doing is essential to having a project well done.

INVEST IN TEAM MEMBER SUCCESS

I believe that caring for your team means looking out for their well-being and making them feel important. By showing team members that you are a resource for support and invested in their success, you will be trusted as a leader.

Every St. Patrick's Day, my husband's graduate students and their families visit our ski house for our "Monte ski weekend," a tradition where a new resident is welcomed through a "rite of passage" team-building program intended to reinforce the group's working relationships. During one year's Saturday night dinner filled with entertaining stories, the program director, Gary, handed out gag "most likely to" certificates, which elicited great laughter. By sharing his knowledge of his students and teachers, the new resident was able to comfortably and naturally get to know the people with whom she would be working.

In another story, one of my favorite self-employed architects Vince and I were working under a tight deadline to submit project plans due on the Tuesday after Memorial Day weekend. On Friday afternoon, I called him to confirm what I needed first thing Tuesday. In a hesitating voice, Vince asked if I could extend the deadline by one day. I said, no, and asked him why he would not be able to produce the plans on time.

He sheepishly replied, "Well, I'm getting married tomorrow, and I rented a house on the beach to spend time with my family who will be here until Tuesday." He actually thought he could produce the final project plans while managing his wedding and honeymoon obligations. At this, I cried out in astonishment, "You are getting married? When the heck were you going to tell me that?" He laughed nervously and agreed that it was a bit sudden. After advising him of the wisdom of first checking with a new wife about working during a honeymoon, I told him to take the week off and have the plans to me the next week.

Fortunately, I was able to revise the schedule to accommodate Vince's honeymoon, although I did wish that he had been more honest with me regarding his wedding plans. In the end, I had to empathize with him. As a business owner, I always want to say yes to my customers. Since Vince was such a big part of our team, it was more respectful to recognize what was obviously more important to him at the time. The lesson here is that there will be times when your best management decision is to take care of your team first.

HELPFUL TIPS

Here are ways to build people care into your project management:

[1]   **Give your team enough breathing room.** Allow team members the freedom they need to collaborate on the details of project milestones and to define their own roles in achieving them.

[2]   **Supply your team with the proper tools.** Create hard-working, detailed schedules that your team needs to stay up to date and focused on the end game.

[3]   **Maintain strong communication ties.** Interact with your team as often as possible. Have lots of conversations and invite powerful dialogue to keep ideas flowing and your team learning and growing.

[4]   **Keep the team in the loop.** Collaborate with your team by reviewing and revising plans as needed and by making sure to inform members on any revisions, including regarding approvals and change orders.

[5]   **Address stressful situations.** Remember that healthcare professionals are overworked and often lack needed resources, which puts them in dire need of keeping things simple. Anything that can make their life easier and less stressful is much appreciated. Keep things grounded with humor and storytelling and it will be easier to engage with your team.

Conclusion

In Chapter 1, we covered the concept of *Healthy Patient,* which covers the most important stakeholder in any PCE, the patient. In this chapter, we learned more about the importance of appreciating, connecting with, and supporting a *Healthy Team.* Chapter 3 presents the third component in the *Health Well Done* approach to building a healthcare environment while ensuring that everyone feels cared for and is engaged from start to finish. *Healthy Project* is the structural backbone of the project process and covers the tools and procedures that will help you organize information, stay on task, and communicate effectively, using a common language to achieve a project well done.

HEALTH WELL DONE

KEY TAKEAWAYS

- Understand and acknowledge a team member's basic need to feel important.

- Make sure every team member is clear on his or her role in the project.

- Projects succeed when teamwork is valued—when everyone places the same importance on a shared goal and is willing to support each other to achieve it.

- Identify each person's working style early on to match skills with tasks and to keep the peace.

- Provide adequate support to participants who might be feeling outside their comfort zone.

- Set up and enforce rules that keep the team feeling psychologically safe.

- Respect the independence of your team members and trust that they can get the job done without being micromanaged.

- Give members the room they need to honor their personal lives and obligations.

HEALTHY PROJECT 3

> "Whatever good things we build
> end up building us."
>
> – Jim Rohn

Healthy Project is the structural backbone of the *Health Well Done* project management system. It is preceded by the commitment to the principles of *Healthy Patient* and the formation of a *Healthy Team* that is clear on overarching goals and objectives, effective in how its members communicate and collaborate, and steeped in the needs of patients, their families, and the caregiving staff. A *Healthy Project* is born out of the detailed consideration of all phases and practical concerns of creating an effective patient-centered environment (PCE)—including the budget, schedule, the management process, healing component, sustainability, WELL Building Standard, and LEED certification—and the optimal application of collective knowledge, skill sets, and techniques. In a *Healthy Project,* activities are executed and managed through a "project life cycle" mapped to the following structure: starting the project, preparing and organizing the project, carrying out the work of the project, and closing out the project. Within this structure are five sequential or overlapping phases—initiation, planning, controls, implementation, and close out. I adapted these key process categories from the Project Management Institute's *Project Management Body of Knowledge (PMBOK)*—the established standard of the project management profession—and modified them to address the unique needs of a PCE project.

Managing a project using the roadmap in this chapter will help your team put the proper structure and documentation tools in place to achieve your goals. This is especially important when considering the "human side" of your project. When the diverse thoughts and opinions of team members inevitably converge, a proper project structure and strong direction will ensure a positive outcome. Strategic controls aid project execution, help focus everyone's efforts, and provide a clear path to the end point.

Given the theme and the hands-on work covered in this chapter, we will dive straight into the Nuts and Bolts section. As you progress through your project's life cycle, keep in mind that a *Healthy Project* cannot run its course successfully without the contributions of a *Healthy Team* committed to working synergistically and within well-defined roles. Whether you are planning out a project or monitoring its progress, try to leverage the unique personality and skill set of each team member, allow them to essentially manage their own project areas, and simultaneously work to uphold the *Healthy Patient* philosophy of addressing the needs of all stakeholders.

NUTS AND BOLTS

A *Healthy Project* adheres to evidence-based design principles (elements proven to improve patient care, strengthen morale, and save money); integrates all healing modalities, both Eastern and Western; goes green when possible; and generates a high ROI (return on involvement). The five phases of project management that I have refined throughout my many years of creating PCEs are the right blend of steps to cover whatever arises during the course of a project. These guiding steps, working in tandem with each other, and in some situations overlapping each other, will keep you from reinventing the wheel or undergoing needless trial and error events throughout the project's life cycle.

Phase 1: Project Initiation

Project initiation is perhaps the most important of all project phases because it involves broadly clarifying and authorizing the project, including formalizing the project's vision, scope, and culture. This is the phase during which a project's feasibility is confirmed and its purpose and requirements established.

The clearer the broader context of your project is the easier it will be to run it day to day and the less stressed everyone will be. Having clarity will help you outline such operational details as aligning the team on goals and intentions, communicating your expectations as the project manager, identifying budget and schedule priorities, defining project controls, directing project implementation, and guiding close-out activities.

Any one of these considerations can easily overwhelm a team. Crucial decisions must be made during the initiation phase before moving on to project planning, design, and development. Specifically, you must define:

1   The project's vision, scope, culture, and intention.

2   The project goals and deliverables.

3   The budget and schedule, or at least how they will be determined.

4   The roles and responsibilities of the project manager and each team member.

5   How communication will be handled.

PROJECT KICKOFF

Project kickoff represents a critical step of the project initiation phase and is when the project manager and team together build a foundation of understanding for how the project will unfold. This includes introducing all the people on the team, arranging a background briefing, gauging a team's baseline expectations, and laying the groundwork for establishing the project's scope and vision, as well as the "culture" under which project tasks will be carried out. The kickoff meeting is also when you can establish your authority as the project manager and set the tone for all things to follow. This preparatory stage will give you and your team the best start right out of the gate.

A kickoff meeting is most useful if it is scheduled early in the project, run efficiently, and wrapped up properly. The rules are pretty straightforward. Begin with your e-mail announcement, in which you explain the meeting's purpose and provide a comprehensive agenda. This will explain what you intend to accomplish and let everyone know that you respect their time. It also encourages participation by providing attendees with information to digest in plenty of time. By the meeting's end, everyone should walk away feeling well informed and clear on responsibilities. And if you have effectively painted the patient-centered "big picture" for the project, they should also feel motivated and inspired to accomplish their tasks.

 ## QUESTIONS TO ASK

To plant the seeds for developing a strong relationship with your team, ask yourself the following:

- How do I want the team to perceive me as a leader of a people-centered project?

- What is my own understanding of the project's vision, scope, and culture?

- How will I instruct the team on group decision making?

- What reporting or accountability measures should I put into place?

- What resources will I extend to the team (for example, to handle conflict resolution, provide advice, etc.)?

As for the setting up and running the meeting, review the essential details (*see* Chapter 2, page 84) and ask yourself the following:

- Who should (or should not) attend?

- Where should I hold the meeting?

- What teleconference tool(s) will best serve this particular meeting?

- When it comes time for everyone to introduce themselves, what three questions will I ask each person to help them understand the role they will play on the team?

- How will I manage the meeting time against the agenda items to ensure a productive and efficiently run meeting that respects my team's time?

VISION, SCOPE, AND CULTURE

Given the ongoing evolution of the healthcare industry and the general rise of the "experience economy," which describes the commoditization of services (*see* Chapter 1, page 20), hospital systems are perpetually scrambling for new ways to serve their patients, making it challenging to pin down a project's vision and scope. Moreover, we managers of building projects are conditioned to act quickly, perhaps not stopping long enough to consider the institutional culture under which we must operate. Clarity in the areas of vision, scope, and culture is vital for avoiding chaos and ensuring a successful outcome, and it also reminds everyone of why the money and effort are being expended in the first place.

If a team does not internalize the project vision (the big picture of everything you would like to accomplish for the *Healthy Patient*), as well as understand and embrace the healthcare system's organizational culture, a crisis management approach can take root. Larry Scanlon emphasizes that, "As the biblical proverb states, 'Where there is no vision, the people perish.' A strong vision makes good business sense and, more important, good patient care sense."[1] Important to add to this wise counsel, however, is that the vision of creating a more meaningful and powerful patient care experience means doing so without overemphasizing process, but rather demonstrating a greater willingness to meet patients and staff where they are. Stick to *Healthy Patient* principles by remembering who the patients are and the experiences they desire. For example, if you want to target patients who are millennials, can you support healthcare experiences driven by engaging visual and educational elements? If you can, you will hook this demographic and keep them coming back.

An accurate scope of a project helps you define the overall intention behind a given PCE by accounting for the culture of the healthcare system involved. Culture, in turn, represents the deeply rooted values of a healthcare system, communicated through a common language that a community can understand.

THE PERILS OF AMBIGUITY

A project that lacks vision and scope and ignores institutional culture will be prone to problems and less likely to succeed in all the important measures. What might happen if everyone walked out of a project kickoff meeting without having a clear plan of action or realistic budget and schedule? Here are two tales of projects that began a bit on the rocky side for this very reason.

When a Tight Deadline Takes Over

I was once assigned to lead the renovation of a pediatric specialty practice. The first meeting of the project initiation phase was also attended by the medical director, administrative director, marketing director, and VP of a foundation also involved. We identified the space to be used, established a schedule, and briefly touched on the purpose of the project and the budget. But we failed to immediately clarify the vision and scope of the project and instead began the project by discussing how we could show a generous donor how we planned to put his gift to the practice to good use.

The first item on our action agenda was to visit other children's hospitals to learn about their programs, their wayfinding system, and their donor walls and showcased artwork. Although the visits inspired our team to visualize ideas for the pediatric practice, we immediately ran into a problem because we did not first consider the tight deadline we were under. So now there we were, having put pressure on ourselves to jump directly into finding innovative ways to design and build the PCE instead of defining our project vision and scope and getting the necessary approval. Sound familiar?

Because we were caught up in impressing the donor, we set an unrealistic schedule. Frankly, there were many other ways to impress. We should have first determined the branding messages that the hospital wanted to communicate to its community of providers and pediatric patients and their families, as well as the pediatric specialties set to join the hospital in the subsequent five years. Our team would have been able to work more efficiently and benefit from better communication.

Thankfully for us, the hospital operated under a Planetree hospital culture model that got us back on track. (*See* Chapter 1, page 34.)

Guided by its overarching philosophy and criteria, and with accompanying administrative support, we felt confident in our decision making. Nevertheless, we had initially moved forward too quickly based on limited information, only to suffer the consequences of lost time, needless stress, and a struggle to hire the right architecture and engineering (A&E) team.

Before kicking off the project's planning phase, familiarize yourself with the institutional culture of the hospital system client. For example, if operating under a Planetree culture, your hospital will strive to meet the full needs of patients, their families, and staff. This could include addressing the issue of burnout among its medical professionals, which negatively affects their quality of life and, in turn, has an impact on patients and their families. It benefits you to know if the system has instituted measures to help caregivers maintain their physical health and emotional well-being, an important strategy for retaining employees, enhancing job engagement, increasing joy in practice, and ultimately improving the quality of patient care.

 QUESTIONS TO ASK

If the organization has a people-centric culture, does the staff have access to space where they can unwind and decompress?

Are staff members encouraged to interact and collaborate with colleagues from other units and departments?

Are healthful food options available to the entire staff?

Speak to the C-suite executives, study the institution's website, find out what the media is saying, visit competing hospitals, and talk with community leaders. If we had listened to the compelling backstory of the children's center, we could have avoided needless delays and stress.

 HELPFUL TIPS

No matter how motivated you are to hit the ground running on your PCE project, internalize the following three pieces of advice:

[1]   **Slow down.** I know that you face pressures and are often forced to agree to ridiculous schedules. Nevertheless, it is in your best interest—and vital to the success of the project—to make a case to the powers that be for working at a manageable pace.

[2]   **Identify a champion in senior leadership.** Every project has a champion. Find yours and meet with him or her face to face to enlist their help. When we were looking to hire the right architectural firm, I met with the pediatric center's chief physician to convince him that we could not meet the schedule until the right professional was in place.

[3]   **Recognize that people process information differently.** If you cannot get a direct answer during a meeting regarding the project's scope and vision, send out an e-mail or call the administrator in charge. Follow up any subsequent discussions with an e-mail that confirms decisions made or next steps outlined.

Winning a Budget Battle

Early in my career, I was assigned by a hospital to build several IT closets and to re-cable the entire hospital, and so I first met with the directors of IT and telecom, Mike and Jim. To detail their vision and scope, they relied on a basic sketch they created using Microsoft's Visio, a diagramming and vector graphics application. After listening to them, I commented that their proposed budget of $158,000 and schedule were unrealistic and that they lacked a set of construction plans that depicted the architectural, mechanical, technological, and equipment details reflecting the true project scope.

I told Mike and Jim that before we could move forward they needed to set aside money to hire an A&E team to draw up detailed plans, but they felt that the step was unnecessary and that their sketch was good enough. Afterward, they contacted me every few days to ask when the project would begin, and each time I responded by saying, "We need a budget to hire an A&E team before we can start." Since my boss supported the idea of hiring an A&E team, I confidently stood my ground.

Two weeks later, Mike and Jim finally agreed to hire the team along with a construction manager who could guide the planning, budgeting, and establishment of means and methods. It was a tough but critical first hurdle to overcome in the project. If we moved forward without a project vision and scope or an approved budget it would have spelled disaster for the project. But having management support gave me the leverage I needed to align these two key stakeholders with the rest of the team.

Next came our kickoff meeting. We invited the hospital's in-house staff, the electrical and mechanical supervisor, the head of safety and security, and the infection prevention nurse. Mike and Jim were not used to working on a multidisciplinary team and, initially, it was hard for them to see the wisdom of involving so many people. They nevertheless agreed to attend.

We began with introductions and then defined roles and delegated decision-making authority. To ensure public safety for patients and medical professionals alike, we had to establish a "360-degree view" of the project's structure (how things would be set up) and the process (how things would be done). We considered the architectural, engineering, and IT aspects of the project, including all the shutdowns, critical patient care issues, and other complex tasks associated with working in a hospital setting. Team members discussed their ideas, brainstormed new ones, and then refined the project details to include every imaginable logistic to arrive at an accurate plan.

During the kickoff meeting, Mike and Jim also heard from experts on the team about the electrical and mechanical requirements for the data center—information that was necessary to properly budget the project and inform the decision-making process. Only then could we wrap our arms around the costs and scheduling details for building the IT closets and running the cables throughout the hospital, among other tasks, and feel confident about the true scope of the budget, which ultimately turned out to be well over $1 million.

Enter the need for CFO approval of the budget, a complication made more complex by the fact that the VP of IT was not convinced that the budget increase was necessary, and who instead wanted us to immediately begin construction. Lacking budget approval, I had to repeatedly refuse his request, and the reason was simple. I have seen project teams get swept away in the moment when hurrying to get things done. Had I moved forward without an approved budget, my team and I would have wound up playing a game of "hurry up and wait." We simply could not properly complete the project under the original budget, and nothing that the VP could say would change that fact.

Fortunately, because they had been involved in the team's open discussions on structure and process, Mike and Jim now recognized the budget deficiency, and so I had two allies with whom I could put together a variance report to tell this important story to the CFO himself. The trick, however, was to get inside his head by presenting the right information in the right way. We wanted to make it relevant to the CFO's perspective and concerns and to deliver our messaging using the right tools, in this case PowerPoint. To properly cast the presentation, we asked ourselves the following questions:

1   What is the story behind the budgeting variance?

2   How important is the project to the CFO's plans for the healthcare system's future?

3   Can we value engineer the project to save money?

4   Can we justify the increase in costs by showing the value proposition to the business over the next three years?

5   Will the CFO be able to find an additional $1 million in other budgets? Can we research and identify a possible source for the funding?

6   If the project must be completed, can it wait until the next fiscal year?

The presentation went off without a hitch. We began with a history of the original budget and how it was calculated, then continued with the facts regarding putting the project out to bid once the plan was completed. Because we knew that the CFO was more of a visual than an auditory learner, we made sure that our information was succinct and graphically driven. We offered a one-page infographic of summarized facts. If he wanted to drill down for more details, he could find them on subsequent pages. Our careful preparation got us to "Yes." Our budget was approved, and the project moved forward to its ultimate success.

Phase 2: Project Planning

More often than not, the overall strategic plan of a healthcare organization will not dovetail with its building or renovation programs. According to The Center for Health Design's Built Environment Network (BEN), many completed projects do not have longevity because they are often initially designed to solve a single problem or fulfill a single need. At one BEN meeting, *Healthcare Design* magazine contributor Debra Levin heard from members who felt that, "Rather than strategy informing design, buildings are dictating organizations' strategy. Or worse yet, after a building is completed, a realization comes that it doesn't actually solve the problem it was meant to solve and the process starts all over again."[2]

How would you feel if your team spent months or years working on a project and spending millions of dollars, only to find out that the finished environment was not patient centered and that the process would have to begin again? "The real world tells us that people will work far harder to avoid a potential loss than they will to achieve a potential gain,"[3] says author Phil Jones, one of the world's leading sales trainers. You and your team have too much riding on your project to become known as the team that missed its project goals, so think bigger and longer term. Taking the right steps will enrich your team's experience, and they might even have fun in the process.

 ## HELPFUL TIPS

To stay true to a high-level strategic plan while designing a patient care delivery model "connection" is key. Guide your client through the process of innovation by soliciting ideas and opinions from all stakeholders—the management team, department employees, construction crew, facilities staff, and end users—and connect them back to your actions. While you are at it:

[1]   **Play detective and dig deeper.** Tour the healthcare system's website and read (or at least skim) its annual report to learn about its mission, strategy, and values, as well as any capital projects.

[2]   **Learn about the healthcare system's reputation.** Find out how the media and community regard the system and its people. Follow major players and influencers (healthcare design expert Sara Marberry and The Center for Health Design are two) and hear what they have to say.

[3]   **Challenge your Healthy Team to define the "environment of care."** Solicit ideas, wisdom, and experiences from people and engage and motivate them

through laughter. Ask a few team members to recount a funny story about something that either worked or did not in their care of patients. Bring up a humorous news story and use its main points as inspiration for lessons learned regarding design, logistics, or the intended patient experience.

[4] **Stick to your Healthy Patient checklist.** Make sure that ideas proposed by the team jibe with your priorities for maintaining a *Healthy Patient* focus.

THINK GOOD DESIGN AND DEVELOPMENT

We can all agree that good design matters, especially with PCEs. But good design does not magically happen. Everyone must be willing to exercise empathy, work collaboratively, and embrace innovation. A good environmental design is the outcome of a process that includes examining a problem from all sides, yet the task need not be grueling or tedious. In fact, solving design problems can be enjoyable when inquisitive minds work together. And when a group is free to arrive at a creative and exciting solution, the process can be a thing of beauty.

Harnessing the Collective Mind

The first step in design and development is defining the problem to solve and the behavior to modify with the new design. The more focused and aligned you and your team are in this regard the better. However, collaboration and learning do not end there. The real work comes with putting everything down on paper. Design development drawings require great detail. An A&E team must spend considerable time digging deep to research such features as room layouts, equipment placement, storage, and all the "behind-the-wall" items (wiring, electrical power, cabling trays, etc.), and present their plan to the rest of the team. Upon review, the team might decide that more space is needed, which entails reconfiguring approved schematic plans.

Changes during design and development should come as no surprise. For example, new equipment models often require larger spaces than older hospital equipment rooms can offer. During the design of an electrophysiology and catheterization lab (EP/cath lab), we found that we did not have the space to adequately site equipment in the operating suite and the control room without restricting the staff's ability to move freely. So prior to drafting design development drawings, our team visited other hospitals that had undergone EP/cath lab installations. They, too, had to deal with small operating suites and control rooms. We saw cables strewn across the floor and tangled cable connection points behind the equipment. In their interviews with us, lab teams expressed frustration with the lack of space in which to move around and with the cabling issues that were an infection control nightmare.

Following this information-gathering phase, our team agreed on two key prerequisites for designing and building our own lab: There would be no cables on the floor and all connections to equipment would be neatly organized. Our room standard included enough square footage to accommodate at least 12 clinical staff members in the operating suite at one time. And while it might look like a no-brainer on paper, fulfilling the directive for a cable-free floor took a collaborative effort that included addressing complex cabling and installation requirements and following protocols for hardware and software that could support eight separate technologies. Needless to say, not everyone agreed on how to accomplish the task, and so we created a mock-up cable bunch—we asked vendors to bring in their cables for comparison purposes—as well as a mock-up room to help the team decide on how to move forward.

Mock-Up Rooms

Given their popularity, mock-up rooms deserve a mention here. These setups—which can represent operating rooms, patient waiting rooms, procedure rooms, etc.—offer tangible "safety zones" of creativity for testing a design concept in its actual physical representation (both in scale and spatial relationships). In a mock-up room, healthcare staff execute simulations and provide the project team with constructive function-based reviews that inform the further development and refinement of an idea.

One of my favorite exercises is to ask physicians and tech personnel to execute a "pretend work" sequence and ask them such questions as: "How would a patient arrive at the lab?" "How would technicians set up the room for the procedure?" "How would the physician suit up?" "What would he or she require of a team to optimally care for the patient?" The information gleaned from this exercise can be surprising. For example, the physician might discover that a table is not properly sited, the medical team might disagree on how to manage a patient's arrival, or the technicians might realize that they have overlooked the installation of a necessary piece of equipment.

Watching end users in action in our mock EP/cath lab and learning how they conducted their work provided the A&E team with indispensable guidance in siting the equipment, especially the lights, booms, and a Zero-Gravity suspended radiation protection system, since space was especially tight in the ceiling and required several group discussions to ensure the proper layout.

Although it is an added budget item, a mock-up room can represent time and money well spent, and simulation results can be documented by questionnaires that serve to justify design decisions. (*See* Resources, page 294.)

ENCOURAGE TEAM CREATIVITY

An important early step in building an innovative PCE is to inspire open, creative thinking in the team, and you can accomplish this by instilling in members a strong, well-defined sense of purpose and a commitment to executing new ideas. In other words, you must give your *Healthy Team* the right problems to solve for PCE end users—patients, families, and staff—and the freedom necessary to solve them.

The sooner you unleash your team's creative force the better, particularly in the first six weeks or so of the project's life cycle, before details are set in stone and tasks begin. This is a special time for brainstorming sessions, site visits, and wish lists; a time when the team can choose which ideas to develop and draft into the final project plan.

There is one cardinal rule to follow when tasking teams with planning: Do not assume that creative thinking just happens. You as project manager must provide a working atmosphere that promotes curiosity, welcomes challenges to the status quo, and allows the unfettered expression of ideas. More often than not, teams are hampered by being forced to consider only evidence-based methods and approaches. Challenge your team members to shift their current mindset and remind them that circumstances are not always black and white. Solutions usually lie somewhere between opposing viewpoints, and the willingness to compromise can yield more than expected.

Give your team members permission to think differently by allowing them to "pretend." For example, how might they plan out a project if the budget were not a factor? What if the team had more time in the schedule? What would it look like if they took a novel approach—for example, if telemedicine were introduced into a location?

As your team develops new ideas, allow participants enough time to thoroughly consider them and to adopt an "OK to fail" mindset. I might introduce an idea to a group by proposing, "Let's pretend that a patient would prefer to see a front desk when they first walk in." The group can embark on visualizing possibilities in new ways and not feel pressured into falling back on the same old planning and design approaches. Being open to implementing new ideas (even for seemingly run-of-the-mill PCE projects) benefits all members of a *Healthy Team*, whether an architect, engineer, IT manager, nurse, administrator, physician, or environmental specialist, among others.

As fun as it might have been, once this creative phase ends, it is time to collectively determine if the plan is on point. If not, revise it accordingly and get any cost adjustments or rescheduling approved. Above all, never assume that the revised plan will be approved. Present all new information to decision makers as soon as possible, since changes can significantly influence the project's design and development stages.

HELPFUL TIPS

Here are tips for keeping the planning phase moving forward with the proper checks and balances:

[1] **Review the project plan.**

Make sure that the details of your project plan align with the project scope and vision.

When you schedule a meeting, make sure attendees have the background and details they need and enough time to review them, make notes, and prepare questions.

Ask the A&E team to review each page of the plan with the team. Discussing project details within the context of the plan helps ensure accuracy.

Have everyone confirm what was discussed in the review meeting by asking them to sign off on the plan.

[2] **Identify outstanding problems and issues.** Proactively keep your team members abreast of concerns and work closely with them on final approvals.

[3] **Address logistics.** Have the A&E team review such logistics details as construction tasks, power and data plans, and temporary area closures, as well as protocols for communicating this information to the hospital community.

[4] **Complete construction paperwork.** Ask the architect for infection control risk assessment (ICRA) precautions or an interim life safety measures (ILSM) plan and submit the material to infection control nurses and safety officers for permit approval. (*See* Resources, page 294.)

TEND TO YOUR BUDGET

Your budget is an important piece of the project puzzle, an accounting benchmark for projecting and anticipating actual costs and a tracker of funds that might come from several sources, including grant- or foundation-based funds and budgeted capital dollars. Keeping tabs on the sources and the overall timing of funding is paramount to good project planning. If financing stops or is delayed, so goes the momentum of the project.

Clients must create comprehensive budgets because it is how they will gain the approval they need to secure funds. Anticipating the line items that can enhance a PCE can take a lot of time and energy, but I strongly urge you to make the effort because a well-considered budget offers creative freedom. When developing a budget, collaborate with team members to customize it, using clear descriptions of assumptions. Letting everyone review and justify line items helps you establish priorities and work from a body of unambiguous information. This will speed up approvals and ensure greater productivity.

Keep in mind that the budget should include preliminary *and* approved budget amounts because if the hospital-approved budget is less than what you projected, you will be protected by having the discrepancy on record. Accurate and timely reporting of cost overruns and savings can also dramatically improve project planning and execution. (*See* Resources, page 295.)

BRING IN A CONSTRUCTION MANAGER

All of us have felt the impact of budget restrictions on our decision-making process or have experienced financial uncertainty. The key driver in the latter is usually construction costs, and it is why I prefer to hire a construction manager when leading a hospital building project. I simply cannot go over budget, not meet the schedule, or deviate from originally specified materials.

Although it might cost you more, bringing in a construction manager as a team member from the start will help reduce overall project costs. Many project managers choose to run the bid process themselves, sending out drawings to several contractors, one of whom will accept the drawings "as is" without allowing much latitude for change. The project manager will then bring in a construction manager to oversee the construction. The disadvantage with this approach is that the manager will likely not be fully familiar with the ins and outs of the project. A construction manager who is on board at project kickoff can provide a reality check on the scope of the project based on its current budget and schedule. He or she can also guide the production and construction methods used, while making sure that nothing adversely affects the delivery of ongoing patient care.

During the project's initiation phase, the construction manager can manage the bidding and construction process, sending out the drawings for bid, selecting subcontractors, and overseeing the work done. As a team member, the construction manager would be fully informed on project details and able to foresee potential issues. And if compensation is tied to keeping the project on or under budget—such as with an agreed-upon percentage on top of subcontractor costs—the construction manager will be more invested in proactively managing the schedule and costs.

HELPFUL TIPS

Ideally, the first construction manager you hire for a project should be the last one you hire. Conduct thorough interviews and never hesitate to ask even the simplest questions. Some additional advice:

[1] **Ensure a good team fit.** Check references, invite the candidate to a team meeting, then solicit team feedback.

[2] **Look for a responsible team player.** The right manager will understand the impact of financial limitations on the project scope and the importance of working closely with the A&E team and subcontractors to establish and maintain clear project parameters.

[3] **Prioritize for a patient-centered strategy pro.** Hire a construction manager who understands PCEs, ICRA and ILSM costs, and has the expertise to plan, price out, and execute the project.

[4] **Carefully consider the services offered and the manner of compensation.** Will the candidate be paid hourly for a limited period, or be hired to work from project start to finish and paid based on a percentage tied to project costs?

CREATE A HARD-WORKING SCHEDULE

Adhering to a schedule for a PCE project is like mapping a long-distance trip. Every exit and connection must be accounted for. A schedule should include not only actual construction tasks, but also any activities that tie into or can be affected by those tasks. Just as a GPS recalculates a route following unexpected construction on a highway, so must a team update and recalculate its moves should an unforeseen roadblock appear during a project.

The good news is that schedules can be as specific and flexible as necessary. Just keep adjusting them and communicate any revisions accordingly, including the potential overall impact of the changes on the project (*See* Resources, page 295, for examples of project schedules.)

Once you have finalized the project schedule on your end, however, it should not be signed off on until everyone on the team has weighed in on how the tasks will be carried out, understands individual and group responsibilities, and is clear on the timeline of each project phase.

As always, even though you might be an expert in healthcare project matters or great with handling clients, you must allow team members to share their wisdom and experience in their areas of expertise. The more invested they are in the project, the better informed you will be. A schedule that is mutually agreed upon makes it easier for team members to commit to tasks, bond with each other in cooperation and idea sharing, and be motivated to solve problems.

LEVERAGE TECHNOLOGY

Will you be relying on project management (PM) software for your project? If not, I highly recommend that you do. For many years, we managed hospital projects using paper documentation and e-mails. A few years ago, we began using PM software to manage millions of dollars in capital projects. Having a repository for project documents—financial plans, requests for proposals, contracts, to name but a few—helped us survive internal audits, maintain best standards and practices, and streamline project controls. Advantages also include saving hours of bill payment and reporting activities and forging good relationships with hospital finance, business, intelligence, and purchasing departments.

When choosing software, consider a platform that provides a user-friendly dashboard for recording financial information and reporting it to management. A tool such as e-Builder construction management software allows clients to stay up to date on financial data and provides customizable, out-of-the-box functionality to cover cost management, funds tracking, schedule management, design review, procurement, compliance, and other related needs. Not only does this keep clients happy by putting some control in their hands, it frees you up as well.

I once worked with a client based in London who was in the United States to build a headquarters. He still held Monday morning management meetings with his London staff at 8 a.m., U.K. time. Using PM software, the client could pull up a project dashboard that displayed financial, scheduling, and other critical project details on one page and in real time. With a comprehensive snapshot of the project's status at his fingertips, he did not need to phone me in the middle of the night with questions or concerns.

As great as technology is, however, the human element is still a factor. If you intend to have your team use a particular software platform, keep in mind that some people are not comfortable with change. The key is to introduce new technology step by step and to be patient because it can take time to adapt to a new system. Strongly encourage the use of the tool, but provide enough time for any necessary training.

DELIVER A DETAILED DESIGN DRAFT

The more details that your A&E team includes in design drawings, the more accurate the budget and schedule will be. For bidding purposes, drawings should include details on infection prevention precautions (required by The Joint Commission), logistics regarding the construction and use of swing space, temporary hallways, loading docks, etc., and be accompanied by a list of requirements and specifics on the equipment that will be installed. Other considerations include outlining the sequence of operations and other information related to facilities management, creating medical equipment preinstallation checklists, and assigning electrical installations. The point is to include any item that will hit the budget or have an impact on your plans or schedule.

Phase 3: Project Controls

Project controls help you manage client perceptions and expectations and give you the opportunity to shine as a leader. Knowing "what comes first and what comes next" is very beneficial. Success, however, ultimately depends on how well you communicate with both your client and team and how efficiently documentation connects all phases of the project process.

Proper controls keep your project intentions, budget, schedule, and execution on track and define the way forward for the team. They can include communication tools, such as a monthly status report that includes schedule forecasting, regulatory to-do lists, team guidelines, workflow processes and procedures, and a budget component that keeps a team accountable and is generally tied to your client's financial health. Status reports keep senior management and other stakeholders up to date on the project, which is critical since their impression of how things are going will have the strongest impact on project decisions, whether it means continued support as the project progresses or the introduction of uncertainty about the patient care model you are following.

During project initiation, be prepared to talk about the budgeting tools and methods you plan to use and how you will apply them toward meeting project goals while still meeting your fiscal responsibilities. If you present decision makers with a budget line item (such as a stereo system) and justify it as upholding your patient-centered principles, the expense will likely be approved. You can also demonstrate the clinical and operational benefits that will result from the patient-centered practices that will be supported by the new space.

QUESTIONS TO ASK

Does the hospital system you are serving have a patient care model in place? Consider the following:

- Is the hospital a Planetree hospital? (You will see the Planetree logo on signage and branding and the hospital listed on Planetree's website.)

- Does the hospital have "Magnet status"? This distinction reflects excellence in nursing and high-quality patient care.

- Check the hospital's standards for a patient care plan.

- Review the system's patient safety standards. It is a good place to start to build on the details of an existing plan.

PROTOCOLS AND RESPONSIBILITIES

There are several important decisions that project managers must make in collaboration with their team members that will define how work on the project unfolds. You must decide on:

[1] **Communication protocol.** Ask your team early on about their preferred method of contact, whether phone, text, e-mail, or memo, etc.

[2] **A weekly meeting schedule.** What is the best day, time, and location that will allow for the maximum participation of your team members? How will you determine people's availability?

[3] **Additional meetings.** Various meetings must be held to keep a project moving, including monthly status report meetings with the C-suite and specialty meetings for deciding on furniture, medical equipment, and other items for the space.

[4] **Management of weekly client meetings.** You will need to assign someone to draft agendas, record meeting minutes, and attend follow-up meetings.

[5] **Generation of monthly status reports.** This responsibility includes documenting all important decisions and any matters that will have an impact on the budget and schedule for any given month.

[6] **The decision-making process and mediation plan.** Identifying the team's decision makers and how decisions will be debated and ultimately resolved early on will keep a schedule on track. Having mediation guidelines in place will allow the team to confidently handle difficult problems. (I talk more about mediation later in this chapter.)

COMMUNICATION MODES

Given how busy everyone is, you will want to find the best way to keep everyone connected and communicating efficiently. In addition to learning your team members' preferences as was noted above, you will want to talk to your team about any PM software platform that you expect them to use to share plans, schedules, budgets, and approvals. Craft a communication plan early on to keep everyone in the loop from the start and include a mediation plan. (*See* Resources, page 296.)

MEETINGS

Ideally, a project manager will schedule and run weekly project meetings to keep a team accountable, organized, and knowledgeable about the project to keep it moving along. In fact, weekly meetings are when much of the actual work can get done. Spending an hour each week to recap agreed-upon objectives and expectations can keep track of team performance.

 HELPFUL TIPS

Unfortunately, for many of us, distractions can often push objectives to the back burner. It is simply the way of today's working world, and some people consider weekly meetings as being interruptive. Here are easy-to-remember actions for muting any complaints:

[1] **Engage:** Make meetings fun and worth showing up for. Begin them on time, be organized, keep discussions on topic, and use visuals—photographs, whiteboard, or PowerPoint presentations—to communicate ideas.

[2] **Involve:** Pick a meeting environment that promotes focusing on the task at hand and sharing information. Quick "stand-up" meetings held in a conference room or department area keep participants attentive and get them quickly back to work.

[3] **Habituate:** Consistency helps people keep their commitments, so meet for at least one hour at the same time and place each week. Set up teleconferences for members who cannot attend in person.

[4]   **Tune-in:** Motivate people to keep their attention on the meeting instead of being distracted, such as by their phones. Try the "champagne rule": Whoever answers their phone must buy the team a round of drinks after work.

[5]   **Accommodate:** Allow team members who are legitimately overburdened by their schedules to drop in on a meeting for a short time, during which their specific topics can be addressed.

[6]   **Clarify:** Ensure that discussions are broken down properly into memorable takeaways so that everyone understands the information being shared and their assigned responsibilities.

[7]   **Prompt:** If you need to boost meeting attendance, seek out help from someone with influence, such as a director who can send out an e-mail mandating attendance.

STATUS REPORTS

Status reports go straight to the C-suite level and will leave a lasting impression on decision makers regarding how efficiently you are managing the hospital's money. Think of your first "formal" status report as being the third time you communicate the status of a project (the first time being when you establish the budget and schedule, and the second time being when you identify a project's critical issues).

Healthcare system clients love making easy decisions, so keep them well informed. Status reports, although work intensive, are worth the effort because they will enhance your professional image.

More practically speaking, if a client is unaware of a milestone, that ignorance could delay your schedule or increase project costs. A status report reinforces a client's responsibilities regarding next steps and allows for timely problem solving. It can also show a client how their actions, or lack thereof, might have adverse consequences.

 HELPFUL TIPS

As the project unfolds, you will have to manage an increasing amount of information. Stay as organized as possible to avoid feeling overwhelmed when it comes time to draft your status report. Here are two very important pieces of advice:

[1]   **Gather information as you go.** Outline your report at the beginning of the month, create a file folder, and each time you encounter a topic that needs to be added to the report, drop the information into the folder. When it is time to create a status report, you will have all the details at your fingertips.

[2]   **Never over-promise then under-deliver!**

Phase 4: Project Implementation

Although a sense of freedom can come from completing design and blueprint plans for a PCE, once you step into the world of project logistics, a new brand of time-consuming work and worry awaits.

After months of planning and setting up controls and getting the right things done, construction is finally under way and the team is completing the assignments set in place at the project's outset. Things are beginning to materialize, and it is a good feeling. You have successfully coached your team up to this point, and it is vital that you do not stop now.

The implementation phase is the tangible outcome of your team's progress, and what I and many other people love most about construction. You and your team have visualized and designed a PCE and now you are all seeing, feeling, hearing, and living the vision in real time. Excitement can run high, but everyone should continue to deliver results, which means that leaders should not stop anticipating problems and resolving conflicts. Stakeholders should be weighing in at different points in the construction. For example, not inviting the nursing staff or IT personnel to check on the progress of the construction prior to close out would be like playing in a championship baseball game without a third baseman and shortstop.

Think about it. What would happen if on the day you opened the space to the end users, connectivity for the medical equipment was inadequate or a supply closet was empty? People who have no idea of the countless hours of work devoted to the project might react to such "shortcomings" by thinking that the project team was incompetent. Your team's responsibility is to stay active from the beginning to the end of the project.

ESSENTIAL TASKS

Many essential to-dos are common to just about every construction project. And since projects can involve multidisciplinary team members, tasks will constantly be added to your list, some of them unexpected. For example, you might be working on a new lab, but the space cannot be opened to generate revenue until the entire medical staff is trained. You must now add "schedule medical and facilities staff training" to your list of responsibilities. Do not be surprised when these tasks pop up, just be vigilant and nimble.

 HELPFUL TIPS

Of the many activities that take place during the project implementation phase, three are of particular importance for ensuring a smooth project life cycle:

[1] **Complete preinstallation tasks.** Before any large equipment is installed, the installer is required to visit the site and approve a preinstallation checklist. Corresponding tasks must then be completed, with you ensuring their proper sequencing. (For example, you would not want the walls to be closed up before all the technology cabling has been installed.)

[2] **Monitor progress.** Compare team and field progress against the schedule and project plans. Try to foresee problems and ask a lot of questions of many people to confirm that your team is on target. I find that if I ask different people the same question, I will get answers that represent different points of view, which can be very helpful in getting the full picture.

[3] **Manage the punch list.** Completing this list of items satisfies the quality terms of a construction contract, making it an agenda priority. It is the A&E team's responsibility to map out a punch list and distribute it to the contractor, project manager, and, in some cases, the end user as soon as is feasible, preferably during the project's implementation phase, since it is the document that subcontractors will follow.

[4] **Complete the punch list on time.** Many patient environments are open 24/7, and if punch list tasks extend beyond the move-in date, the subcontractor could face scheduling conflicts, which can lead to additional labor costs and potentially affect or disrupt the delivery of patient care.

COMMUNICATION STYLES

Creating the best possible PCE means having a team that works well together in an environment that is emotionally, intellectually, and psychologically safe. Remember, not all communication is verbal. It pays to know the four basic ways in which human beings communicate:

1   Verbally, through words and language

2   Vocally, through changes in the tempo, inflection, volume, and tone of one's voice, and in sounds

3   Physically, through gestures, eye contact, and other nonverbal reactions

4   Emotionally, through feelings, such as those elicited by a moment in a story

Not everyone is great at every type of communication. Some people are shy and hesitate to speak up. Being aware of different communication styles, including gestures and nonverbal reactions, will help you know what people are thinking and feeling. For effective communication during project meetings, be as specific at every turn as possible, since details affect the clarity of the information conveyed. I remember a meeting during which our team had decided on the delivery date of a bidding set of plans. When the day arrived, no one knew the next steps. We had not discussed how many sets of plans would be needed, whether they needed to be in a hard copy or electronic format, or how we would make them available to bidders (via e-mail, on a Web-based platform, etc.).

Another example showing the importance of team communication involves distributing submittals. Typically, the architect on a project is the first to receive them and has overriding approval authority. But you might want to consider simultaneously distributing the submittals to the architect, engineer, and client to allow enough time for review and approval. The architect would still maintain authority, but a coordinated distribution method could speed up the process.

In both of these examples, a team would still need to adequately discuss even the simplest tasks, which can have people chasing their tails. Subpar communication can cause chaos and waste everyone's time.

INSTITUTIONAL COMMUNICATION

Having the wisdom to know the many ways in which your project plan can be affected is of paramount importance. Whether you are a project manager working as an outside consultant or on the hospital's staff, ask the right questions at the right time. Good communication and proper timing mean everything in a hospital setting, where decisions such as temporarily shutting down power to an area or closing off an oxygen outlet can have serious consequences.

Although we are trained to see the big picture, it would be a mistake to miss the small details because they can have a profound impact on getting your project completed without a hitch. As the leader of the project team you will find yourself communicating on many levels. The most effective way is by putting yourself in another person's shoes. To the best of your ability, you should try to learn the ins and outs of the hospital, since an insider's perspective will help you to identify what needs to be communicated to the appropriate parties.

In his business book, *Running the Gauntlet,* Jeffrey Hayzlett writes, "No one is going to die from the changes you make in business." But he then says of a manufacturer of life-saving equipment, "Please do not cut corners and ignore important details while you are executing change."[4] Nowhere else might this be more applicable than to work performed in a hospital setting. We once worked on a CT-scan room and needed to shut off the oxygen. The valve was connected to a riser, which meant that oxygen shutoff would affect other areas of the building. Until we had shut down the entire riser, we could not shut off the CT room's oxygen feed.

We met with people from each department located along the riser, including the operating room and respiratory medicine departments, to communicate the plan. We took the precaution of supplying each area with oxygen tanks in case of a problem.

Although the procedure took extra time and involved more staff, it ensured the continued proper care and safety of patients.

You will find yourself asking many questions. Do it in a way that shows people you are authentically invested in doing the right thing. Listen closely and connect with them, such as by encouraging them to tell you stories (*see* Chapter 4). It will help you determine the precautions needed to responsibly complete tasks and get you closer to project completion without delays.

Once you have gathered enough background information on important needs, develop a detailed plan and present it to the people heading up facilities, security, and nursing. Once they approve logistics and dates, communicate the information hospital-wide. You can assign this task to a team member, but it is your responsibility that it gets done. Next comes signage. If you need to close a hallway, for example, you will need to draft an ILSM plan and an ICRA plan. (For information on managing hospital logistics, including on checklists, signage, ILSM, and ICRA, visit www.ASHE.org.)

EQUIPMENT VENDORS

I have worked with many equipment companies, and some are better than others. There are companies that, based on their hospital contracts, come up short when it comes to the in-person participation of their representatives, particularly with respect to weekly project meetings when important decisions are being made.

HELPFUL TIPS

I prefer to work with vendors that are team players and are motivated to get things done right. I suggest that you make sure to do the following:

- Ask to review the equipment contract or purchase order. The purchasing department staff or the director should have this document, which specifies deliverables and delivery dates.

- Ask the equipment vendor if a representative will attend weekly project meetings. If not, ask the vendor to specify the amount of time to be spent with the project team and in what capacity.

- Provide the vendor with a full description of the project tasks to be completed and review the details with them to make sure there is no misunderstanding. You might need to revisit the contract to determine if there will be an added cost for vendor involvement on the team.

PLUG-AND-PLAY EQUIPMENT

Equipment companies might not have an allegiance to your specific team because they are likely working with many other customers at the same hospital. For example, a salesperson selling a CT-scan machine might first visit the director of radiology, a physician, and a technician. Say the director of radiology then contacts the purchasing department for budget approval. The department would negotiate pricing and draw up a contract. If the salesperson has positioned the equipment as a "plug and play" (the removal of an older piece of equipment and new equipment replacement), the facility or IT personnel involved might not be invited to discuss equipment installation or the impact that the purchase might have on the budget or facility.

For example, what if the installation and construction costs turn out to be well over $550,000, an amount that would undermine the radiology department's budget? Now you have a situation in which the director has purchased a CT-scan machine but must wait until the next fiscal year to actually receive it. Moreover, if the director leaves the radiology department before then, the incoming director might not be familiar with the purchase and installation of large equipment.

If your project involves installing several pieces of equipment, consider hiring a medical equipment planner to serve as a liaison and help with the many logistics involved. Just make sure you have confidence in the person you choose.

 ## HELPFUL TIPS

Here are important things to remember regarding planners, equipment delivery, and installation:

[1]   **What payment covers:** If your planner is not local, their fee should cover weekly meeting attendance. Make this and other expectations clear.

[2] **Equipment delivery/storage:** The planner should arrange for any needed storage facilities and deal with movers and loading dock personnel. If you are not working with a planner, make sure you have a trusted storage facility under contract that can store equipment until its installation in case it arrives on time but there is no place for it. Equipment companies will not take on this responsibility.

[3] **Equipment removal:** Do not assume that the purchasing department will automatically require a company to remove existing equipment before an installation. If this detail slips through the cracks and is your responsibility, it could cost your budget $5,000 to $10,000, depending on the circumstances. (*See* Resources, page 296.)

MEDIATION

Despite your best efforts at good management and communication, problems will arise and need to be settled. All too often, problems can be exacerbated if they are not addressed directly or when people document a response or resolution through e-mail to cover themselves. This unproductive approach can easily backfire and add fuel to a fire. You should have a mediation plan in place that involves direct interactions.

I have a general rule that once a problem arises, we stop e-mailing and get on the phone or meet in person. Emotions can be hard to gauge through an e-mail message and wording can be misinterpreted. Present the problem using graphics and visuals, if appropriate, so that everyone understands the nature of the situation. This action will save time in the long run. Knowing that there is recourse for handling communication issues or other bumps in the road gives team members the confidence to face issues head on and actively seek solutions. (*See* Resources, page 296, for more on mediation.)

Working together directly has additional benefits, such as quashing rumor mills. Once, during a walkthrough of a job site, I spotted a painter painting a wall yellow. I asked him why the wall was yellow, since that was not the color specified on the plan. He replied that the director had told him to paint the wall yellow. This is a simple example, but with many clients can come many wrenches thrown into your project. The sooner you get your team in the habit of confirming details with the primary contact, the better your chances are of staying on track.

STAFF TRAINING

It is never too early to plan for training physicians, nurses, technicians, and also environmental services, security, and facilities personnel. Even if this step is not part of your official responsibilities, training will undoubtedly affect your project opening. For example, the EP/cath lab that I talked about earlier housed eight integrated advanced-imaging technologies. Before move-in, every physician, nurse, and technician had to be trained and certified to work in the room. So we listed "training completion" in the project plan as a prerequisite for opening the operating suite and allowing it to generate revenue.

Depending on what it covers, training can take place at different times and vary in length, and so you must factor it into your schedule. For example, environmental service people should be

HEALTH WELL DONE

trained before the final project is delivered, since they will be responsible the final cleaning of the PCE before the staff takes occupancy. Facilities personnel are responsible for completing inspections and must be trained on all mechanical systems. If team training and departmental training are properly built into a project plan, the project hand-off will be smooth.

Phase 5: Project Close Out

Close out is the transition period between project hand-off and "day two work" (tasks that are outstanding after the staff has taken over the space). Exiting the project involves critical steps that must be completed. You must inform your client of any issues that will affect move-in, develop a process for facilities training and space turnover, work with the accounts payable department to reconcile the budget, process all final invoices against approved contracts, and receive all releases and waivers.

Since how you close out a project has consequences, get in the habit of beginning the process sooner than later. When everyone knows what is expected of them and requirements are detailed early on, there is less likelihood for disagreements. Close-out requirements—punch list items, warranties, reconciliations, etc.—should be built into any request for proposal sent out to architects, engineers, construction managers, and medical equipment vendors, with client requirements made explicitly clear. A detailed spreadsheet will keep everyone clear on budget items and accountable from a financial perspective.

TIE UP LOOSE ENDS

Even in a perfect project management world where everything is miraculously on track, there is plenty of work to be done in anticipation of completion. Ask yourself the following questions and track the information on your schedule, making sure to cover it in your project meetings.

 QUESTIONS TO ASK
_____

[1]   **Utilities:** Do I need to schedule utility shutdowns or arrange for internal permits?

[2]   **Move-in schedule:** Have I scheduled departmental moves and communicated any physical disruptions, such as hallway closures, to the hospital administration and the staff who will be affected?

[3]   **Walkthroughs:** Will the medical equipment company representative need to walk the site to determine delivery methods, cabling needs, and preinstallation inspections?

[4]   **Inspections and approvals:** Will you need to obtain state approvals or certifications, carry out building department inspections, file for a temporary certificate of occupancy (C of O), schedule staff and facilities personnel training, and obtain approvals for the loading dock or security approvals for garbage dumpsters and deliveries?

KEEP COMMUNICATING

As the project winds down and everything begins to fall into place for the move, keep your team on its toes with plenty of ongoing communication. Require that the punch list be completed early on, even if your architect and engineer believe that the contractor might not be able to do it. Once the space is open to patients and staff, it will be nearly impossible to have unfettered access to complete the punch list, and work performed at that point can have a potentially negative financial impact.

For example, a punch list item could be implementing infection prevention precautions, such as an ICRA plan, which could lead to additional labor costs, including overtime. Since inspections and C of Os might be required before opening a space, it pays to keep current on city and state code requirements so as to avoid needless delays.

ATTEND TO INVOICES

The timeline of healthcare system capital projects generally corresponds with the system's fiscal year. If invoices for payment are not submitted soon after a project's completion, an important window for payment might close. If you wait until year's end when unused budget money is taken away, you could have trouble pulling money from another budget. Remind vendors to submit their invoices and lien waivers as early as possible and send out reconciliation letters to confirm that no follow-up invoices will be submitted.

Keep your project budget up to date and it will be easy for you to reconcile all potential exposure items and pending change orders. (Last-minute needs will always pop up.) Stay calm and focused, but move at the speed of light to complete the space for use to lessen or eliminate extra work later.

DOT THE "I'S" AND CROSS THE "T'S"

Before a client moves into a new space, a "substantial completion letter" must be signed, which certifies the owner's agreement that the contractor has completed the contracted work (minus any punch list items) and is entitled to a reduction in their retainage. Follow your state's rules on this matter. For example, in Connecticut you can withhold 2.5 percent of the total contract until the punch list has been completed.

You will also need to prepare a close-out package (*see* Resources, page 296 for more information) for the client to sign off on. It should include:

1   A financial close out

2   As-built drawings

3   Operating manuals

4   Punch list signoffs

5   Department of building and fire department
    inspection signoffs

FEEDBACK AND LESSONS LEARNED

Once you have wrapped up close-out tasks, you might think you can begin another project, but no project should be considered formally completed without gathering end-user feedback and holding a "lessons learned" meeting. The ideal time for this is after the staff and patients have used their new space for at least two weeks. Typically, the entire team will meet with the staff in the new environment and encourage them to talk about how they are managing in the space and about any patient reactions they have observed. Detailed notes are taken and distributed to the team and administration to serve as a record and reference for subsequent projects.

 ## QUESTIONS TO ASK

When interviewing end users, I like to use my SPA storytelling method (*see* Chapter 4, page 182) to collect the right information. I might ask the staff the following questions:

- Can you tell us a story about your first workday in the new space?

- How about a story about your first patient's impression of the new space?

- Did everything go smoothly or was there an operations issue or other issue? Can you tell us a story about how it affected patient care?

- What do you like, or not like, about the new space? Is there any aspect of the new environment that you want to know more about?

Assessing the finished PCE is an important activity, not only to ensure that the space is working for everyone, but because it will be the first time—and perhaps the only time—that you will hear that your team did a good job. One related story that comes to mind is about a nurse in the EP/cath lab who had to operate a camera that was unfamiliar to her. The large piece of equipment had to be rotated into place for use. Thinking with a *Healthy Patient* mindset, the architect had incorporated color coding into the flooring to mark the camera's location, and the nurse was grateful for this safety detail.

In a *Health Well Done* project, you will doubtless hear stories from staff and patients about how your team went above and beyond to make true improvements for the users of the new PCE. These are details that the C-suite should know about.

Press Ganey, a patient experience consulting firm, believes that measuring patient satisfaction—through such tools as the Press Ganey survey or HCAHPS hospital survey—and soliciting patient comments can provide the C-suite with valuable data on the patient experience in a newly built environment. But before pages of data hit administrators' desks, consider having the first post-project impression come from an actual tour of the completed project. It will give you the opportunity to acknowledge your team members' hard work and collaboration. The administrators' reactions to the PCE will speak volumes but remember to graciously welcome all assessments and comments. If, based on feedback, there are changes that you can realistically make before exiting the project, then make the changes. It will leave a good impression on the decision makers and help you secure the next project.

Respect the End User

With almost every project that I have worked on, I have seen feedback reinforce the team members' passion, purpose, and strong spirit that made success possible. Witnessing the results firsthand affirms to them that the effort was worthwhile. From a practical standpoint, the comments they hear give them ideas on what to do next time and enrich their wisdom and experience, helping them professionally and personally. This is especially important, since the vision, scope, and complexity of a PCE project are unique to that project and shaped by the time and resources allotted to it.

But equally important is being sensitive to whether the organizational culture has been served by the new PCE. One of the most powerful aspects of any culture is its ability to adapt to changing circumstances. Some cultures are nimble and resilient, bending effortlessly with the winds of change—others not so much. Throughout my 24 years of project management work, I have observed that people generally do not like change and need time to acclimate and manage any resulting stress. Give individuals the time to react and do not take anything personally. Be forewarned, however, that unfavorable reactions can occur at any administrative level and for seemingly trivial matters.

Years ago, our team was charged with relocating a large accounting firm into a new space. The partners' offices decreased in size from 750 square feet to 250 square feet and could no longer accommodate couches and sitting areas. The executives who had previously enjoyed convenient parking on the same floor as their offices now had to park across the street. Three days before the move, one of the partners confronted me, upset about her smaller office and the furniture placement, and then demanded that immediate changes be made. I calmly explained to her that changes could only be made two weeks after the official move-in date. Until then, all plans were frozen.

This did not go over well with her. She immediately responded with, "Let me remind you, I am a partner in this firm and you are an outsider who is being insubordinate." In hindsight, I should have kept my mouth shut and let her speak her mind uninterrupted until she got everything out of her system. She just needed to vent, and I was a convenient target. I gave her my business card and asked her to e-mail me a list of her changes. I told her that I would take care of things in two weeks, and I worked with her to make sure that everything was done. She eventually adjusted to her new surroundings, and even became happy about it all.

This end user's reaction is not uncommon and shows just how powerfully people can become attached to their work environments. A change in their surroundings or work process can distress them. This is a time when *Healthy Patient* especially comes into play. Understanding and accommodating healthcare staff and patients requires going beyond simply planning out and executing a great PCE build.

In another example, imagine a 20-year-veteran healthcare professional who has walked her unchanged environment day in and day out arriving at work one morning to find everything changed. How can it not be a shock to one's system? In my experience, if you give people enough time to occupy the new space, nearly everyone will gradually adjust to it. In fact, some people wind up wondering why they felt stressed in the first place. This is why a two-week adjustment period should be built into your *Healthy Project* plan. The allowance shows respect for the perspectives of the end users and gives you the time to manage reactions and accommodate change requests, all while staying on schedule and on budget.

CELEBRATE

No project is truly complete until you personally recognize and thank your team and celebrate the end users. A project takes hard work and a commitment to see it through, yet all too often everyone's focus is on completing the punch list. A project team that has performed well deserves to be celebrated.

Arrange to have everyone tour the PCE as a group, and this time with fresh eyes. As you walk with your team, be direct about pointing what you accomplished together. Formally congratulate the team as a whole, but also highlight each person's unique contributions. It is up to you to make time for this, and there is no better way to cap things off than with a well-deserved party, during which everyone can not only pat each other on the back but also decompress and resolve any shared experiences in a relaxed, upbeat setting.

A good time to throw a party is soon after the "lessons learned" phase when the team is feeling especially good. But plan early and check in with management staff to avoid having your event conflict with any formal celebrations in the works by the healthcare system's foundation or a specific department. As for the manner of celebration, let the nature of the project dictate it. Will it be a coffee and doughnuts affair on move-in day or a formal ribbon-cutting event attended by dignitaries, honorees, and perhaps the media? Will your project team even be invited? If not, hold your own event accordingly.

Conclusion

Professionals who facilitate the building of PCEs are committed to ensuring that the project they have planned out, designed, and executed is one that can best keep a patient community healthy and a healthcare system's staff happy and productive. It is a tremendously difficult job, and I should know after having spent many years leading PCE project teams. As this chapter has outlined, there are many moving pieces to a project and everyone has a hand in the process. Applying the principles of *Healthy Project* in concert with those of *Healthy Patient* and *Healthy Team* under the *Health Well Done* project management approach will help you stay on track, encourage collaboration through all phases of the project, inspire innovative thinking, account for staff and patient perspectives, and make the most of the lessons learned.

Now armed with the knowledge of how *Healthy Patient, Healthy Team,* and *Healthy Project* work individually and together, you will learn how to enhance your team's communication skills, creative process, and problem-solving ability—through the art of storytelling. In Chapter 4, I delve into the power of applying this ancient skill to project management and how my simple SPA approach can give you a winning advantage.

O━ KEY TAKEAWAYS

- Project controls help focus team members' efforts and provide a clear roadmap to end goals.

- A *Healthy Project* relies on a *Healthy Team* that is committed to working synergistically and within well-defined roles.

- Project initiation is a key project phase. The clearer the project's purpose and requirements are, the easier the tasks will be, keeping stress levels low.

- A project kickoff meeting is most productive if planned ahead, run efficiently, and wrapped up properly.

- Collaborate on budget development, customizing line items and drafting clear descriptions of assumptions.

- Good schedules promote individual commitment, team bonding, cooperation, idea sharing, and problem solving.

- Connecting with stakeholders is key to staying true to a high-level strategic plan while designing an optimal patient care delivery model.

- Creative thinking requires an atmosphere of curiosity, challenges to the status quo, and free expression of ideas.

- Communicate, communicate, communicate.

- Always remain calm.

THE ART OF STORYTELLING

CHAPTER 4

"We are all storytellers. We all live in a network of stories. There isn't a stronger connection between people than storytelling."

— Jimmy Neil Smith

It seems appropriate to open this chapter on storytelling with a story. My grandmother emigrated from Ireland to the United States in 1910. She married and gave birth to seven children. She was a strong woman, whose Irish husband—a tough New York City firefighter—passed away before I was born, and she was left to raise her family largely on her own.

Sunday dinner was an important tradition that remained a constant throughout the years as the family ranks grew with the addition of spouses and grandchildren. If you ever had the pleasure of entering my grandmother's home for dinner, you would first see the dining room, with its large, welcoming table, and then smell the rich aromas of meatloaf, soda bread, and apple pie wafting from an Irish kitchen. With a pretty apron tied over her Sunday dress, my grandmother would stop whatever she was doing to come greet you with a smile before sprinting back to where she had left off in cooking or setting the table.

She always sat at the head of the table during dinner, asking each of us to tell her our "stories of the week." It was her way of finding out about what everyone was doing and if there were life lessons she could teach. She would also tell her own stories about the old country and her family, as well as make sure to visit the children's table to ask each grandchild for his or her story to make them feel special and loved. The conversations continued long after the food had been eaten and the dishes washed.

My grandmother's use of storytelling was both a process and an art and required no tools. At their core, her stories were vehicles for passing down important information and strengthening "tribal bonds," and they helped create a home environment that was warm, inclusive, and loving. This tradition profoundly influenced my life and is one of the reasons why I have always enjoyed opening up my own home and breaking bread with guests. When we share the day's adventures during convivial gatherings, we can vicariously experience events and reinforce our connections to each other.

We Are Biologically Wired for Stories

Many historians and psychologists believe that storytelling is what defines our humanity and binds us together. The great thing about storytelling as a communication tool is its ease of use. We are all natural storytellers—it is literally in our DNA. The human mind is hard-wired to think in specific story-based terms that resonate with us and help us make sense of our world.

Doug Stevenson, founder and president of Story Theater International, believes that stories stay with us because we process them as images. And not just as still frames, but as motion pictures that run simultaneously through our mind's eye as we might listen, for example, to a neighbor recount skiing for the first time, or as we lie on the couch riveted by the narration of an exciting spy thriller audiobook.

Well-told stories exert a profound influence on our everyday lives, regardless of whether the story is a TV news piece or an ancient tale of Norse mythology. In a *Fast Company* magazine article, Jonathan Gottschall, author of *The Storytelling Animal,* quotes psychologists Tim Brock and Melanie Green, who state that "entering fictional worlds, 'radically alters the way information is processed,'" and that "our attitudes, fears, hopes, and values are strongly influenced by story."[1] With all of us having told or been told stories throughout our lives, who can argue that they touch hearts and minds and elicit emotional reactions that influence the way we see the world and our place in it? But what is it about a story that makes it so powerful?

Neuroeconomist Paul J. Zak, who studies why stories have the effect on us that they do, has pointed out two critical aspects of a story that make it resonate: "First, it must capture and hold our attention. The second thing an effective story does is 'transport' us into the characters' world."[2] This "narrative transportation" allows listeners to experience emotional stimulation, which is the very foundation of empathy. And what is the neurochemical responsible for narrative transportation and empathy? Oxytocin.

Zak's ground-breaking research involves how oxytocin affects behavior. His lab discovered that, "when the brain synthesizes oxytocin, people are more trustworthy, generous, charitable, and compassionate." He states, "I have dubbed oxytocin the 'moral molecule' and others call it the love hormone. What we know is that oxytocin makes us more sensitive to social cues around us. In many situations, social cues motivate us to engage to help others, particularly if the other person seems to need our help."[3]

It is easy to see the potential power that storytelling can have in the context of creating a patient-centered healthcare environment (PCE), where empathy and compassion underpin the delivery of care. Artful storytellers, whether they are project managers, vendors, or end users of a PCE, can sway thinking and change perspectives, which can prove indispensable for motivating individuals involved in a project to commit to shared goals.

Perhaps one of the most important advantages of storytelling is how stories persist and endure, as evidenced in the countless archetypal tales that have survived across the millennia in various iterations. Facts can be anchored in more lasting and impressionable ways with an interesting, relevant tale than with a bare-bones presentation, the latter of which can be misinterpreted, inadvertently altered, or simply forgotten, making storytelling a genuinely effective addition to your project management toolkit.

Storytelling Versus Mere Data Collection

It is not hard to see how storytelling can play a role in the planning, designing, and building of a PCE. Simply put, given the tremendous impact that your project will have on the many stakeholders who are connected to it, it is paramount that you go beyond simply collecting data about your project because data alone will not tell the complete and compelling story. You must contextualize the data through storytelling to facilitate engagement, ensure effective messaging, and see a greater return on ROI (return on involvement)—all necessary for creating the PCE that is "well done."

One could, empirically speaking, consider a project meeting place, such as a conference room or a hardhat area, as being a data collection site filled with all the information required to draw up a blueprint, determine the equipment needed, or figure out which walls can stay or go. Facts like these must of course be collected and shared among team members to move the project along. But here is the problem: Patient-centered healthcare is not built on cold, hard data. It follows the precept that caring for human beings inescapably involves the hearts, minds, and spirits of everyone involved.

This means assuring project team members that their input will be well received, their perspectives will be acknowledged, and their unique insights and ideas will have the chance to constructively inform how a PCE is built to have a lasting, positive impact on patients, families, and staff. One of the best, most natural ways to support a *Healthy Team* in such a way is to allow members to share their experiences and wisdom through real-life characters and situations.

Storytelling can enhance brainstorming and convey innovative concepts, which helps a team better leverage project information. Not many people are profoundly affected by simple facts and figures presented in a sterile context (such as a PowerPoint presentation). But tell people a compelling personal story and you can attach meaning to data and stand a greater chance of having listeners internalize and memorialize your intended takeaway points.

You might also be able to guide emotional reactions from your team in ways that forge or reinforce strong working bonds, trigger new thinking, and inspire action. For example, stories can bolster a group's confidence in having identified the right problem to solve and also foster a collaborative environment that supports fresh thinking and the experimentation needed to reach a successful outcome.

Storytelling can reinforce PCE priorities by helping the teller and the listener gain an understanding of the healing that takes place in a healthcare environment. (In Chapter 1, I talked about how an understanding of healing is the counterweight to the practical backbone of a build process, which sometimes overrides other important considerations.) Storytelling is one way to properly balance process to make sure that the concepts of healing and wellness remain in the project equation. To refresh, imagine a scale with the "human aspect" of a project on one side and process on the other. The *Health Well Done* approach to a project "well done" relies on maintaining a balance between the two aspects and not sacrificing one for the other.

In this respect, storytelling shines because it grants the team creative license to innovate (and not be afraid to fail). The best ideas come out of many minds working together. Just think of the diverse perspectives, expertise, and knowledge represented in a project team, all of which can be disseminated through a simple story that serves as a resource for brainstorming and problem solving.

Stepping Outside Oneself

We spend too much time planning our own actions and not enough time listening and observing others, and this is why storytelling is such a productive exercise. Storytelling requires active listening. People must consciously put all other thoughts and concerns aside and pay attention to what is being told, which sets the stage for group-based inquiry and transformative creativity. By telling and hearing stories, team members step out of their individual spheres of subjectivity and gain a greater awareness of what others are thinking. When teams work in this holistic way, the impressions shared transform into queries and problems to be tackled.

The benefits of storytelling cannot be underestimated. Creativity researchers have discovered that, in addition to solving existing problems, groups that are highly creative are also good at spotting problems that might have otherwise gone unnoticed, which is certainly a plus when it comes to building PCEs. Furthermore, storytelling opens the door to unambiguous thinking, since what we say in a story is more often what we mean. When an "honest" story is told, the ideas, insights, and discoveries it yields are that much more valuable, since crystal-clear revelations can feed innovative thinking.

Perhaps one of the most important benefits of storytelling in the context of encouraging team participation is how it can help establish a trusting and safe atmosphere for sharing wisdom and experience. Motivational speaker Kelly Swanson believes that, "Trust is about connection. ... When we know you as a person, we connect to you. Now we listen to what you say."[4]

WIDEN YOUR STORYTELLING CIRCLE

The advantages of storytelling can extend beyond connecting with project team members. Long before any blueprints are completed or demolition begins, you must be clear on the C-suite's perspectives and expectations, as well as on how the hospital tribe (management and staff) will react and interact when it comes to dealing with emergencies, planning, external compliance issues, agencies, government rules and laws, and other responsibilities. You must identify and acknowledge their concerns, respect their sense of autonomy, individuality, and style, and uncover their sources of pride or frustration. In short, every person who will experience the PCE that you are creating has a unique and valuable story to tell.

The front lines of patient care delivery are where perhaps the greatest opportunities can be found for connecting with stakeholders and uncovering project priorities. As the project manager, you must be sensitive to the different struggles involving patients, families, and staff. This means being open to hearing stories of heartache, happiness, worry, hope, or disappointment, and of how ordinary people cope under extraordinary circumstances. These poignant accounts can originate from every corner of a healthcare system—a doctor's exam room, an X-ray room, hospital pharmacy, or even a construction site. Origin does not matter. What does matter is how much better a PCE could be designed if we relied on the richness of a family or staff story.

For example, nurses can offer a treasure trove of insight and information, yet all too often they are not consulted. I saw this firsthand during my time as a patient with cancer, and it made me realize just how far-reaching of an impact that a team's decision making can have on even the simplest of details—in this case, a recliner.

After undergoing an abdominal surgery that was similar to a C-section, I was transferred to the hospital's "mother/baby wing" and given a private, relaxing patient suite that included a sleeping bench for a guest, large windows, a nice bathroom, and TV access to the C.A.R.E. Channel (featuring peaceful nature scenes and soothing music). My stepdaughter Alexa commented on how she had never seen such a spacious hospital room.

One day, the nurse asked me to sit up in a recliner that happened to be a model approved by my project team. As she assisted me into the chair, she warned me to "be prepared" to have the chair flip back. She assured me that she would try to soften the landing, but the sudden impact I experienced not only frightened me, it also hurt. As I had lain in the recliner, I vowed to have the chairs changed out as soon as I returned to work. Why was our team unaware about this "torture" chair and the danger it posed? Because no one had sought the opinions of the nurses. The nurses knew—nurses know all—yet we failed to take advantage of their knowledge regarding this one small, yet very important detail.

And that leads to another important point about storytelling:

A "LOUSY" STORY IS A GOOD HEALTHY PROJECT STORY

Everyone has heard their friends wax poetic about wonderful doctors and exemplary healthcare facilities. But stories of praise are often upstaged by tales that sway us in the opposite direction, or perhaps even scare us into never stepping foot in a certain provider's office or hospital. There are plenty of lousy stories out there that deter other patients, and they can circulate prolifically— especially on Facebook or other social media outlets—to wreak reputational havoc on institutions. Yes, stories can open up the imagination and offer details that people can relate to, but the power of a story is a sword that cuts both ways.

When I was a patient, I was asked to follow up with my urologist one week after my hospital discharge. Upon arriving at his office, I was taken aback by the inappropriately dressed front desk staff and a space that lacked cleanliness and reminded me of a boys' locker room, with sports memorabilia on the walls, dark hallways, and dirty, outdated chairs. While waiting for the doctor in the exam room, I looked around at what was an infection control nightmare. I imagined Brenda, our infection control nurse, whispering in my ear, "You need to leave this place now!" I found myself questioning the competence of the doctor, and I could not get out of there quickly enough.

Eliciting difficult stories might take some probing, since some people can be shy about telling them. But lousy experiences, if properly leveraged, can have great silver linings because they provide team members with the chance to conscientiously correct problems that they would never want anyone else to experience. I find that medical professionals, in particular, are very protective of their patients and often exhibit an attitude of righteousness about turning things around. This commitment can greatly benefit a project.

Bear in mind that in certain situations, such as a room filled with C-suite executives, your team members might hesitate to share the truth about an awful experience in fear of being viewed as having a negative outlook. A project manager should counsel the team that the best way to tackle this challenge and avoid the perception of negativity is by simply speaking truthfully—and not too emotionally—about a bad experience and to follow the story with a helpful solution or two.

Stories are our way of telling everyone about our experiences and can drive our buying decisions more than any other source of information. If we do not tell these "lousy" stories at our project meetings or in the hospital board room, they will inevitably surface and be discussed on social media—perhaps out of context—making it of greater benefit to shed a bright light on them for resolution and to ensure a *Healthy Project.*

NUTS AND BOLTS

The act of storytelling is not only indispensable for information gathering, it can be an enjoyable team building activity that allows participants to function as both information conduits and teachers. So how do we capture the essence of experience through story and then apply that information to our design of a PCE? We begin by being willing to apply our own storytelling experience to the project at hand. For example, those Sunday dinners with my grandmother made me feel comfortable with creating storytelling environments in the workplace, the techniques of which I will now share with you.

The SPA Approach

Communication can be one of the hardest things to master, but storytelling can be simple and straightforward. And I have made it easy for you with what I call my SPA approach, which stands for [S]tory, [P]oints of the story, and [A]pplication of the points. A story is told, the points of the story are identified, and the team makes these points actionable by relating them back to the project. The SPA approach uses storytelling to identify the right problems to solve and protect project ideas from being quashed too quickly without proper consideration.

How the SPA approach works: During meetings, for example, the project manager might invite someone in a group to tell a story, after which the group would identify the story's main points and then apply the insights gleaned to an aspect of the project. It could involve determining the logistics for properly running the project, designing a space, diagramming a workflow, considering ideas on patient care, or addressing infection prevention. This is a golden time, when you can get "the whole story," including any previously unknown factors that might pose, or are already posing, an issue for your workflow process. Although the choice of what story to tell is up to the participants, certain guidelines should be followed to ensure that the exercise is fruitful and stays on track in terms of time and message.

KNOW YOUR AUDIENCE

Storytelling opportunities should be seamlessly integrated into your team's project activities to not appear forced. Still, you might feel a bit uncomfortable with asking your team to tell stories. It takes practice, so give yourself time to get good at it and remember that no two stakeholders are alike. For example, you might meet with a group of "left-brain-dominated" thinkers who depend on raw data and compiled lists. They might pose a challenge for you since, interestingly, "right-brain-dominated" thinkers tend to be better at recognizing patterns and extracting meaning out of seemingly unrelated events and information, as occurs with storytelling.

You can accommodate left-brained stakeholders by asking them to tell you a story about a patient using an exam room, and then have them plot out directly on the design plan how patients would walk, or be wheeled, to the reception area and what would happen along the way. This "visual story" helps data-driven thinkers understand the patient experience, and it gives everyone the chance to ask questions to move the story along.

"GO TO THE VIDEOTAPE"

Everyone on your team has likely watched a football game and heard this phrase. But they probably have not heard it during a project meeting. Use it as a memorable "trigger phrase" to prompt your team to visually "replay" a PCE end-user experience. For example, while sequestered in an exam room waiting to be seen, where would a patient be seated? On a chair or on the exam table? Would he or she be looking at a magazine or checking their phone? This exercise helps your team picture the patient or staff member experience in a way that fosters greater attention to detail.

PROVIDE STRUCTURE AND A FORMAT

You can also turn a story about a patient into a case study. Many people in our industry understand how case studies are constructed and used in research and therefore might feel comfortable working within this format. Start by providing a story example. Determine its structure—the who, what, where, when, and how. Note the characters and how they are feeling. Identify any obstacles, conflicts, or challenges, and then ask your team to describe what they would do in a character's place. Next choose one participant to tell his or her own story using the structure that you outlined and provide feedback on the story elements. As you work through the case study with your team and begin identifying the points of the story and their application, remind everyone to be open-minded about possible solutions beyond seemingly obvious ones. (*See* Resources, page 297.)

KEEP EVERYONE ON TRACK

Provide storytelling participants with time limits to keep everyone focused and on point. Give team members 2 minutes to come up with a story involving a patient or a staff member. (If the participant is new to the healthcare industry, they can share a relatable story from another industry.) Each person should tell a story to the group in 3 minutes or less. Feel free to use a fun timer, placed where it is easily seen, to keep the atmosphere relaxed and friendly.

COACH YOUR STORYTELLERS

Help storytellers tell the best story they can by advising them to "keep it real" with specific people and events. Remind them to include plenty of details, describe sensations, and recount the reactions of story characters. They should also try to communicate in clear, succinct sentences and wrap up any loose ends at the story's conclusion. Equally important, participants should remember that not all language is verbal. They can rely on more than one mode of communication to add emphasis or interest to a story. As covered in the previous chapter, page 150, communication modes include:

1   Verbal: words/concrete language.

2   Vocal: tempo changes, inflection, volume, and attitude.

3   Physical: movements and gestures, eye contact, and nonverbal reactions.

4   Emotional: expressing an emotion connected to a moment in a story.

DISCUSS THE STORY SHARED

Work diligently with your team to uncover the many possible lessons (points), both logistic and interpersonal, and use them to brainstorm a better way (application) to consider an issue at hand or to improve the project. Do not let even the shyest team member off the hook. Everyone should participate by digging deep as storytellers and being unafraid to ask questions about the visual imagery painted for them.

The beauty of storytelling is that it need not be a formal exercise. It is a widely applicable tool, effective in many project settings, so use the SPA approach whenever and wherever you think it will work. In just about any situation you can simply say, "Tell me a story about how that happened," and let the group describe the character's experience.

THE SPA APPROACH IN ACTION

A story does not have to be riveting or full of dramatic or unusual events to be valuable. Even simple, seemingly everyday events at a healthcare facility can yield useful insights. What follows are examples of applying valuable information gleaned from a story to solving an issue or addressing a concern. I begin with the story that initially convinced me of the impact of storytelling on a PCE project, and which inspired me to incorporate the SPA approach into my *Health Well Done* project management system: My own story.

Cathy's Story

On the day I arrived at the cancer center to undergo chemotherapy, I was an emotional wreck. I did not want to be in my own shoes. Thank God my husband had accompanied me because were he not there I would have never crossed the threshold. After exiting the elevator, I locked eyes with a female patient wearing a beautiful head scarf. Her eyes told a story of sorrow and pain, yet they also shone a toughness. As I walked forward in search of the front desk, a curly haired receptionist named Page greeted me. Her caring attitude and high-energy personality immediately made me feel more at ease, and she was instrumental in explaining the treatment steps before me.

Although my experience with Page was a reassuring one, what followed was not as pleasant. I was eventually called into a darkly lit, makeshift waiting area located directly opposite the front desk. I say makeshift because the room was technically a small closet connected to the blood lab, which itself was dingy and crowded. As I sat there having my blood drawn in full view of passersby, I wondered how my phlebotomist managed to be so wonderful to me in a working environment that was dated, dirty, and lacked natural light. I made sure to remember that day.

In fact, throughout my eight-month-long, life-altering treatment experience, I mentally chronicled every physical step I took and professional encounter I had. I collected valuable information about myself, about the staff caring for me, and about the healthcare system as a whole. Being a believer that things happen for a reason, I knew that important lessons would come out of every step of my journey to wellness.

After returning to work, I was committed to applying my newfound insights toward improving PCEs and work processes. In January 2012, I was assigned my first PCE project: the renovation of the reception area at the cancer center where I had undergone chemotherapy. When I met with the architect on the project team, Vince, to view the approved schematic plan, I knew that I could wield the power of my personal story to persuade the team to make necessary revisions to the plan, increase the budget, and extend the schedule.

You might think, "Big deal. Does story really matter?" Take it from someone with more than 70 PCE projects under her belt. Being in the role of "end user" left a lasting impression on me, not to mention my family and friends. The observations that I walked away with—everything I saw, heard, smelled, touched, and tasted—and the emotional reactions they elicited, compelled me to approach facility improvement based on a patient's perspective from then on. I wanted my team to vicariously experience what I did so that they, too, would be as motivated as I was to improve the project.

Here were my goals for the reception area: I wanted to ensure that upon their arrival to the cancer center, patients could immediately locate the front desk and be greeted by an upbeat, cheerful receptionist (like Page) whose primary responsibility was to inform patients and put them at ease. It was important that the front desk, blood draw waiting area, and lab all flowed together in a well-designed, connected way. I also wanted the blood-draw waiting room to be private and comfortable and for the lab itself to feature private stations that were spacious, soothing environments and offered plentiful natural light.

These were ambitious goals, so I had to carefully consider how my story could help me make a case for them. I needed to etch a certain image into everyone's mind and make it clear to them what they needed to do. To ensure that my story would have maximum impact, I asked myself the following questions:

1   **Who did I want to influence?** I needed to make an impression on not only the project team, but also on the director of the cancer center.

2   **What messages did I want to convey?** I wanted the team to revise the schematic drawings to have the front desk installed directly across from the elevator. I did not want the waiting room area to be visible from the hospital's main hallway, but instead have it and the blood draw lab relocated together to a site overlooking the atrium, which had more natural light. Finally, I wanted to give the lab a "facelift" by brightening up the surroundings and increasing efficiencies for the phlebotomists.

3   **What did I want my team members to think?** I wanted them to hear my patient story and my impression of the facility where I had spent so much time and to use that information to increase their knowledge about the space.

4   **How did I want my listeners to feel—about me, about themselves, and about the healthcare system's brand?** I wanted them to remember that our hospital was a Planetree hospital that cared enough about the patient experience to make the necessary corrective changes that would uphold its commitment to serving patients, families, and staff.

5   **What did I want my listeners to do as a result of my story?**
    I wanted them to take action by revising the project plans,
    schedule, and budget.

My goals for telling my story served as my outline, and my
preparation paid off. I connected with my team members,
touched their hearts, and witnessed tremendous empathy in their
eyes. They had stepped outside themselves to gain a greater
understanding of what it was like to fight cancer.

Considered under the framework of the SPA approach, the
storytelling points that the team subsequently arrived at for this
particular renovation proved indispensable:

1   **Communication is key.** A front desk, or signs pointing
    to a front desk, should be immediately visible to patients
    upon their entrance to a PCE. Patients should be promptly
    greeted and given clear instructions on next steps, as well
    as an exit strategy following their visit.

2   **Dignity, respect, and aesthetics are paramount.** A blood
    draw lab should offer privacy and ideally be exposed to
    natural light.

3   **A happy staff makes for comfortable patients.** Patients
    are apt to feel confident about the care they are about
    to receive if the person who provides the care appears
    comfortable in the working environment. A project team
    should strive to understand how an environment affects
    staff interactions with patients and solicit ideas for
    improvement from these professionals.

Bobby's Story

In this story, a team member recounts how an oversight during a janitorial activity could have posed deadly consequences for a patient on a life-sustaining machine.

Bobby, an electrical supervisor, had received an urgent "stat" call to the second-floor hospital wing, where a patient's ventilator had stopped working. He discovered that the problem was a tripped circuit. After getting the equipment working again, he decided to determine the cause of the malfunction. As Bobby was leaving the hospital floor, he noticed a floor buffer parked in the hallway. Knowing that the equipment ran on 220 voltage, he checked to see if it was plugged into a dedicated 220-volt outlet. It was not.

As Bobby told this story during one of our project meetings, he went into character mode, using movements and gestures to illustrate what the patient was experiencing, including reenacting the patient holding his throat and gasping for air. By acting out the event, we vicariously experienced what he experienced from the time he received the nurse's call to his "Aha" moment in the hospital corridor. Although the event itself was nothing to laugh about, the way Bobby recounted it made us pay attention to the information being communicated. We were all in. His detail-rich story communicated his dedication to patient care and the seriousness of ensuring that such an event never occurred again. The team arrived at the following priorities:

1   **Keep everyone up to speed.** Facilities, clinical engineering, and environmental services personnel should participate in team meetings to learn about hospital maintenance equipment, and the project team should be aware of

the proper mechanical systems required to allow staff members to do their jobs well.

2   **Plan for every detail.** A standard should be established to require a dedicated and clearly designated 220-volt outlet installed every 75 feet throughout the length of a patient unit hallway to allow the safe, efficient use of the floor buffer. In addition, environmental services staff should be educated on the proper use of the outlets.

3   **Empower staff.** Hospital staff greatly respect and care for the well-being of their institution's patients and understand that their jobs play a big part in patient care and safety. The project manager and team should acknowledge the group's needs and equip them in ways that help them work optimally.

Pete's Story

Pete, a project superintendent for a construction company, was in charge of renovating two operating rooms (ORs). At the project kickoff meeting, the team discussed creating a physical barrier to separate the construction crew from the clean hallways and active patient areas. After experiencing pushback from the OR staff regarding logistics, Pete landed on an idea based on a previous project he was involved in at a different hospital, where the construction crew was separated from the ORs, hallways, and patient areas by temporary walls built between the OR rooms under construction. Pete went a step further by removing a large set of windows located directly across the hall to create a new dedicated access point. The construction crew could enter the work area and receive deliveries via the enlarged opening with its attached scaffolding without disturbing ongoing patient care.

Using the SPA approach, the team applied the story points gathered from Pete's observations to solving their own logistical issue:

1 **Think proactively.** Anticipating issues can keep the "aggravation meter" needle out of the red zone and a project on track to meet schedule milestones.

2 **Be persistent.** Healthcare professionals do not always understand tasks associated with construction. They might push back on ideas they think would disrupt patient care. Keep pushing for a solution using a story that illustrates a satisfactory solution. It will show healthcare staff that you are on their side.

3 **MacGyvering is OK.** In healthcare construction, you must sometimes be inventive and unconventional in your problem-solving approach. Not arriving at a quick and simple solution can have consequences on your schedule and budget.

Beth's Story

Beth was a new radiology department manager at Stamford Health and the champion assigned to our team, which was tasked to build the Darien Imaging Center. During our first project meeting, Beth mostly observed, although it was not long before she became an active team participant. She took great pride in her role and was excited about creating something new for the community. She shared her big-picture idea for the center by telling us a story about the fears, wants, and needs of patients who come for imaging services. She even acted out the roles of patients, families, and staff members to make sure that we knew how they felt.

For example, she detailed how patients arrived and were discharged, how long they waited to be seen, and the kind of privacy they required. She also talked about her staff and what they needed for self-care, such as a break room with upbeat decor and plenty of sunlight, convenient parking, contemplative artwork, and an outdoor sitting area for nice days. Beth also involved her staff in the planning process by inviting them to attend project meetings and be very actively involved in making decisions about functionality, logistics, and finishes.

Thanks to her involvement in the project from start to finish and her stories, our team was able to create an environment that reflected the needs of everyone concerned. The return on involvement was an empowered staff of professionals who felt that their concerns and input held weight, which in turn motivated them to invest in their work environment. In fact, at nearly a dozen years old, the Darien Imaging Center hardly looks its age, which I attribute to the great pride that the staff has demonstrated for it. As for the project team, the SPA approach yielded the following points:

1   **Involve front-line professionals.** Always bring in the medical professional end users at the beginning of a project for gathering information and documenting their ideas. As a project progresses, plans might change and issues arise. If discussions are not ongoing, you might miss running revisions by front-line staff and consequently miss the mark in building a people-centered environment.

2   **Enlist an "insider."** Find the shining star in the organization (there usually is one) who can serve as your champion— someone with the vision, passion, and energy to make necessary organizational changes come to life.

3   **Seek an ROI**. Your return on involvement will rely on how well you listen to staff and end users regarding their roles, functions, and needs in the new space. Applying their suggestions to the built environment goes a long way in helping staff take "ownership" of, and care for, the space over the long term.

Patient Testimonials

Having a 360-degree view of the patient experience can help your team zero in on creating the best possible PCE. Think outside the box by reaching out to the healthcare system's marketing and patient relations departments for testimonials that confirm your project planning theories on providing the best patient experience. Testimonials or patient satisfaction survey results are themselves stories about what matters most to patients, families, and medical professionals. They can be about achievements and triumphs, or about necessary improvements. Whether describing great or not-so-great experiences, testimonials are invaluable. Use them responsibly and follow HIPAA regulations, including protecting patient identities.

I have used the "testimonial turned story" tool in many of my workshops, especially when working with construction companies. For example, we used customer testimonials for a company that had a good track record of solving tough problems, and for one hospital in particular (*see* Resources, page 297, on patient testimonials). Using the SPA approach on the testimonials, I identified the characters of the story (the construction superintendent and the project manager). Once the team identified the points of the story, everyone could move forward with the project design, including thinking up ways to enhance the patient experience and plan logistics.

For one hospital project, the scope included laying carpet, painting, and installing refurbished furniture in three separate entrances: the main hallway entrance to the hospital, the neonatal intensive care unit (NICU) entrance, and the ICU entrance. Our team worked with the hospital's marketing team to find testimonials that referenced experiences with the NICU and ICU. We were interested in hearing accounts from the medical staff about the waiting rooms, hallways, and entrances, and about visitors' experiences with locating and entering the units. We learned about the characters (patients and families) and their behaviors, as well as what they found useful or comforting and what they complained about.

Armed with this information, our team created a plan that included closing off the three entrances in phases over a three-week period. With each closing, we set up a temporary entrance or waiting room to provide a seamless alteration of the flow of patients with minimal stress. This was a big logistical deal because it involved coordinating with several departments. Providing easy-to-spot signage was key since patients and families had to arrive at an entrance located on the other side of the campus. (Imagine the extra stress imposed on people who are in crisis mode if they cannot navigate quickly to an ICU or NICU.)

As we read through testimonials, good ideas came to light. One particularly successful idea was the installation of directional signage that featured dedicated graphics and colors. If visitors needed to reach the NICU, an image of a blue mouse showed them the way, while a purple elephant would guide them to the

ICU. These visuals also helped hospital greeters and security personnel provide clear directions to others.

In closing, also remember that storytelling can take various forms, including the written word appearing in many formats, such as on hospital websites and Web videos and in advertising and print collateral, among other sources.

Delegate Storytelling

I am sure that, like me, you are always juggling to get everything done. Why not pique your team's curiosity about storytelling to gather information otherwise missed on a busy day? For example, if I cannot seek stories, I might tell my project superintendents to ask their team members to tell stories. Here is one example of how this might work:

Imagine that a hallway needs to be closed off overnight. The superintendent might say to a nurse, "I need to shut down this hallway between 10 p.m. and 3 a.m. Is that OK?" The nurse might respond, "Yes, go right ahead." Why would this be a problem? By asking a "yes" or "no" question, the superintendent has likely just blocked himself off from receiving important information on the goings-on in the hallway, which might pose trouble for him and even risk work coming to a screeching halt.

In other words, the true story could be that during that time of night, patient meals are being delivered via the hallway to be closed off. If meals cannot be delivered, a complaint about the closure will travel straight to the executive office, which will request that the hallway be opened and that future construction work be better planned out so as to not impede patient care.

Work stoppage costs time, money, and trust. Losing the trust of medical professionals or environmental services staff, who could become less cooperative with you, can have significant consequences. Moreover, since stakeholders might lack experience in building PCEs, it is important that you word requests in an open-ended storytelling format. If a person is uncomfortable with telling you a story, approach them in a different way. For example, the superintendent could phrase an initial question in a way that invites participation, such as by showing the nurse that he recognizes that her knowledge is valuable: "Can I ask you to do me a favor and tell me the backstory on the second-floor hallway?" If the nurse agrees, questions that follow could include:

1   "Has this hallway been closed off before?"

2   "Who uses the hallway during these hours? Will deliveries be made tonight?"

3   "If I were to close down the hallway tonight between 10 p.m and 3 a.m., who do you think would be affected, and in what ways?"

4   "Are there alternative routes that people can use in the meantime?"

5   "What else should I know to minimize any inconvenience and make sure patient services are not interrupted?"

Make no mistake, your goal is to get the "truth and nothing but the truth" from the storyteller to uncover what is most important in their day-to-day work in the space.

Conclusion

Storytelling is both a process and an art and requires no tools. Its power lies in the fact that data cannot tell a full, compelling story of a given situation because it lacks context and the human element. With each story told, your *Healthy Project* will be ever more enhanced with a greater ROI, thanks to a better engaged *Healthy Team*. Your messaging will be more comprehensive and effective because it will be based on informed decision making. Finally, you and your team will very likely enjoy an increased level of personal satisfaction in the work you are doing, as well as forge a long-term connection to your ultimate goal of creating a PCE that reflects a *Healthy Patient* mindset.

Now that you have learned the benefits of taking a creative storytelling approach to maximizing your project management efforts, it is time to switch gears in Chapter 5, where you will learn how to creatively manage a project's unexpected twists and turns.

KEY TAKEAWAYS

- PowerPoint slides, charts, spreadsheets, and other data-rich sources of information cannot tell the entire story when it comes to identifying PCE end-user needs, determining project goals, and uncovering and resolving issues.

- Storytelling is a powerful tool that can help your team embrace the concept of patient-centeredness in the context of their own roles and responsibilities, but also help everyone think outside themselves.

- Use the SPA approach to storytelling: Identify the components of (S)tory, the (P)oints of the story, and the (A)pplication of the points to address goals and issues; enhance PCE design; iron out logistics; ensure a positive patient experience; and support infection prevention measures.

- Storytelling is easy and fun, requiring nothing more than an open mind and an atmosphere that is supportive, collegial, and encourages sharing.

5

WHEN PROJECTS
GO AWRY

"It always seems impossible until
it is all done."

— Nelson Mandela

Parents often ask the age-old question, "How can
my children each be so different?" Most will admit
that despite adoring them all, there are "easy"
children and then there are children who give us
a run for our money. Projects can be the same
way—they are our babies after all—with some being
easier than others. And there will always be those
projects that keep you on your toes and make you
put in extra hours just to keep your sanity. The basic
"personality" of the project can force you to keep
two steps ahead of it just to keep it on track.

Sometimes getting a project done will seem impossible, a bit crazy even, and things will begin to spin out of control. There you are as the project manager, working hard to exhibit the traits necessary to uphold the principles of a *Healthy Patient, Healthy Team,* and *Healthy Project*—a sense of humor, persistence, openness, high energy, a proactive and responsive attitude, the ability to build trust within the team, and the willingness to share and receive wisdom. But the project is going off the rails, even facing failure. What next? Never fear, because the great managerial traits that I just mentioned will see you through even the most difficult challenges.

In this chapter, we examine case studies of typical problems that can arise from internal and external forces at play, beginning with issues that fall under your oversight and involve process or team dynamics, followed by examples of outside problems, often unexpected, that can complicate your efforts. We begin with one of the most common issues project managers face.

The Pie-in-the-Sky Schedule

Although few people would consider project scheduling to be easy or enjoyable, a certain satisfaction and confidence comes with working under a realistic timeline that is clear, detailed, and features well-considered dates and milestones. Nevertheless, scheduling a project can present a Goldilocks dilemma: A poorly populated schedule can hinder a project, while an overly ambitious one can pose its own set of logistical and morale-dampening problems. A schedule that is "just right" is one that a team feels confident about and includes project tasks that are achievable from both logistical and time-management standpoints.

I once worked on a lab room project where the hospital client was pushing to be first to market. A new physician had joined on to run a new program, and our schedule was very aggressive. Not recognizing the risk underlying such a challenge could set a team on a course for an inevitable chain reaction of missed milestones and chaotic attempts to recover.

While a first-to-market competitive focus is understandable, a looming, pressure-filled deadline, with its need for speed, can lead a team to lose sight of its intended design and end product. I had already learned this lesson from serving as an observer on a previous project, a hybrid operating room (OR), that was run for the most part by my boss and another project manager. The schedule had been quite unrealistic, but instead of pushing back on it, the project manager pushed the team members forward in a highly unorganized fashion that also forced them to work overtime. The space was finally ready to receive equipment, but as the truck transporting it pulled up to the loading dock, the equipment fell off the back of the truck. Unfortunately, it was too damaged to install. So despite the team's hard work, it missed the most important project deadline and everyone experienced failure. Had the project manager pushed back on the untenable schedule from the outset, the outcome might have been different. Yes, the equipment might still have fallen off the truck, but enough time would have been built into a reasonable schedule to resolve the unexpected issue and still meet the completion deadline.

Applying what I had seen occur in the OR project to the lab room project, I made sure to assemble a knowledgeable team that included the lab's new physician and her radiology technician. We covered our bases by focusing on the goals of ensuring proper functionality of the lab and control rooms for the staff and of optimizing healthcare delivery for the patients. The team turned out to be one of the best interdisciplinary groups that I have ever worked with, and together we set a manageable schedule by seeking everyone's input, including from the construction company. It was the right way to move the administration away from its initial, unrealistic schedule and to agree with our justifiable dates and milestones. Rather than allow an already bad schedule to slip and let chaos take over, and then have to explain why milestones were missed, we gave ourselves the breathing room we needed to properly complete the project on time and in a transparent fashion.

Who Needs a Budget?

How many times are we all handed a project with an unrealistic budget? This happened to me during the build of an outpatient primary care clinic. After a "behind-the-scenes" deal was cut between a real-estate broker and a hospital administrator, our team was handed a budget to build out the space at a cost of $70 per square foot, an impossibly low amount.

Unfortunately, the broker was not experienced enough to make an informed recommendation to the hospital administrator, in part because of not knowing what questions to ask. Instead of consulting with administrative personnel who were familiar with hospital standards and compliance issues, he assumed the work could be completed for the amount quoted. Had the broker asked the right questions, he would have learned, for example, that the exam rooms needed to be equipped with sinks, a costly undertaking since most buildings lack the infrastructure to support the number of sinks required.

When a budget does not reflect the scope of a project, there can be delays in hiring and paying people, ordering and installing equipment, and in other workflow tasks, not to mention a risk to the assurance that appropriate quality and safety measures are being taken. And since the project stops once the money stops flowing, you should not pull the trigger on any work until a comprehensive budget has been approved by the powers that be. Without administrative approval of funding, you risk serious consequences.

Do not kid yourself. You cannot start a project without a budget in place.

Lack of Team Participation

Projects can easily fail if a team cannot work together to effectively plan a project. Again, it cannot be overstated that your efforts as a leader are only as good as the strength of your team. Unfortunately, you might not always enjoy full cooperation from everyone involved in a project, and when stakeholders hold the keys to the kingdom, any inside agendas can disrupt even the best intentions.

I saw one such situation unfold during the build of a radiology reading room consisting of six offices, each of which was to be equipped with dimmable lighting, an adjustable desk, and a new chair. Simple, right? Well, the answer is no. We were under a hard deadline to move the staff into the new space, yet from the start, the chief radiologist would not attend project meetings, which posed a problem because he was a key decision maker. When he failed to show up, his staff froze with indecision.

Projects maintain their momentum with timely decision making. Otherwise work slows down, stress levels rise, and the mission becomes unclear. At this point, you must implement what I call the "decision rule": If the primary decision maker does not attend project meetings, the team will make the necessary decisions.

This rule did not sit well with the chief radiologist, who claimed that he wanted to participate in decisions regarding the design, functionality, and furnishing of the space. Unfortunately, he still could not understand the importance of timely feedback and decision making on important matters, leaving his staff feeling unsure about the ideas and answers they were providing us. Given our strict schedule, I moved forward without the chief's input.

What worked in my favor was making sure that I still met with him several times during the course of the project to discuss plans and get him on the record regarding his poor meeting attendance. My detailed notes provided the justification I needed to garner the COO's support of my solutions and forge ahead to finish the project.

Unfortunately, the chief radiologist's lack of participation continued to undermine our efforts. Once the staff had moved into the space, one of the radiologists complained that the chairs were uncomfortable. To accommodate the department, we met with the furniture dealer, who offered to switch chair models if we returned the original chairs within a week. We brought in two new models for the radiologists to try out—even creating a spreadsheet to tally their preferences—and gave them two days to decide.

Five people out of seven approved the same chair model; however, their signatures had been crossed out in the spreadsheet.

The chief radiologist reported that everyone, except for one dissenter, had signed off on a different model. What I discovered was that the chief had "corrupted" the vote by warning everyone that they would regret picking the model of their choice. So rather than stick to the majority vote, the group decided not to decide. I told the chief that if a replacement chair model was not chosen by the next day, the original chairs would stay, and that is exactly what happened.

As you can imagine, the chief radiologist was not my biggest fan. Every time he saw me in the hallway thereafter, he would stare at me as if his team's indecisiveness had been my fault. Although my boss acknowledged that the project team had done all it could, it did not change the fact that to this day the radiology staff is still using the same chairs.

Chair selection might seem a trivial detail to some people, but in my experience it happens to be a very personal choice given the amount of time we sit while at work. I will never forget a pharmacy renovation that included replacing chairs that were more than a decade old. Although the staff was comfortable with them, they were dirty and torn, and the infection prevention nurse, Brenda, was pressuring the team to replace them. Meanwhile, the COO had a rule that when a department was renovated, it was important that the space actually look renovated. In this case, we decided to time things a bit differently by bringing in sample chairs early on and asking everyone to weigh in.

We made sure to drive home the need for new chairs. During one meeting, Brenda stood up in front of everyone and said that the existing chairs had tears and needed to be replaced for safety reasons. Everyone signed the "chair choice sheet." At the next meeting, we reminded everyone that the old furniture would be discarded. We made sure to state this because not everyone likes to part with items they have grown comfortable with in their environment.

We thought we were golden, until chair delivery day. We had instructed the furniture dealer to remove the old furniture as soon as they made the swap. But one of the pharmacists, Joan, who had known all along that the old furniture would be removed, would not let him take her chair. The next day, I noticed Joan's old chair back at her desk and began rolling it out of the space. She followed me, demanding its return. It was not a comfortable encounter, particularly since I was not responsible for easing the staff into accepting the change. Even though I knew I was backed by the COO and Brenda, I stowed away the chair, knowing the issue was not yet resolved. I was right. Joan initiated a department-wide petition to bring back the old chairs (that only a couple of people signed).

At the next project meeting with the entire team present, the department chairman recounted the disruption caused by the chair drama. Looking me in the eye, he asked me to return the chair. Without saying a word, I left the room to retrieve Joan's chair, along with a new chair. Just the sight of the two chairs side by side made the chairman gasp. Joan's chair looked as if it had once resided next to a burning barrel under a highway overpass. Without further debate, I was told to discard the old chair and the matter was settled.

The lesson here is that as a project manager you must recognize that a lack of stakeholder participation can come from a fear of change. Find creative ways to convince people that change is good.

Communication Breakdown

In matters of project management, communication must be deliberate and specific. Unfortunately, people today are distracted more than ever and might also not have all the resources they need to do their jobs. Never assume that everyone has seen and internalized the information you disseminate. Project details can be complex, multilayered, and require constant clarification, whether through an in-person meeting, conference call, or e-mail exchange.

Despite your best efforts, you will find yourself settling problems of miscommunication. For example, some people shy away from addressing issues directly, believing that an e-mail or a text is enough to document a resolution that will cover their tracks. This approach often backfires because the tone of a message can be misunderstood or its content misleading or incomplete, which adds fuel to a fire. A mediation plan should always be put in place during the project kickoff meeting. (*See* Resources, page 296.) If a problem is exacerbated by vague or ineffective e-mail communication (which itself presents challenges), then move on to face-to-face meetings or phone calls to confront the problem head on. To ensure clarity, accompany your presentation of the issue at hand with easy-to-understand graphics and visuals. Hard-working supportive materials will save time by succinctly highlighting the nature of the problem and encouraging team members to acknowledge it and seek a solution. Let me show you why.

DEALING WITH MISCOMMUNICATION

It always amazes me how the smallest problem can turn into a larger issue when communication is not timely. We once had a room ventilation problem, where the measurement of an exhaust fan showed an inadequate airflow. Our efforts to resolve the issue resembled a game of telephone, where one child whispers something to another child in a circle of children, and by the time the message reaches the last child it is unrecognizable.

First came a string of e-mails about identifying the ventilation problem. Our facilities department interpreted the messages as putting the blame on the construction company, which in turn took a defensive position and locked horns with the department. Two weeks later, we still had no solution, so I called a meeting with the mechanical engineer, the facilities engineers, the construction company, and the staff that used the space. Low and behold, the reality was not what we had surmised from the string of e-mails, and we were finally able to get clarity on the problem, which actually had to do with the main hospital's HVAC equipment.

By inviting everyone to a problem-solving session, I motivated the parties involved to do their research and present their case in an atmosphere of collaboration. It is amazing how a meeting does not have to turn into a showdown or blame game, but rather an opportunity for everyone to commit to resolving the issue.

There are additional benefits to face-to-face interactions. They help stop the rumor mill (that can spread untrue project-related assumptions). During a walkthrough of a job site with three other team members, we uncovered a serious oversight regarding the installation of a lead-lined wall. Immediately after the walkthrough, the department director phoned me in a panic, saying that she had just heard that the wall had to be demolished and rebuilt from scratch, which would set back the schedule.

The rumor did not stop there. It traveled up to administration in a flash, and the next thing I knew I was standing in my boss's office trying to figure out what had happened. Instead of being able to concentrate on resolving the original issue—which we eventually determined was not as bad as the director had assumed—I was forced to spend valuable time dealing with an out-of-control rumor. The lesson here: Minimize the likelihood of assumptions and misinformation snowballing into major headaches by instructing your team to seek confirmation on project matters from primary sources instead of third parties.

Should anyone balk at the time required to meet with others in person, my strong advice is that you not buckle under such resistance, even if you think that phone calls are more convenient and productive than in-person meetings. Believe it or not, communicating by phone has its own downside, which is that you are not guaranteed a person's full attention. People on a call might be driving in heavy traffic or sitting at home multitasking. How can you compete with a dog barking, children fighting in the background, or spotty phone service?

I was once on the phone with an architect who agreed to sketch out a solution that we had discussed in detail. When I followed up with him, he wanted me to remind him of what I needed in the sketch. How could he not remember that he was the one who said the proposed design would work? I think it was because I did not use visuals during the original call. The architect did not look good in this case, but were the crossed wires his fault or the result of suboptimal communication? The best way to prevent this problem is to follow up your calls with a written confirmation of key discussion points, decisions, and next steps.

BUT IF YOU MUST CONFERENCE CALL...

Think about the many conference calls that you participate in weekly. Have they all been productive? Are you confident that everyone on the call is clear on what is going on? Some participants might unintentionally derail the conversation with side questions, while other people stay silent because they are unsure of what to say or ask for fear of sounding uninformed or because their attention is elsewhere.

Unfortunately, disengagement is unproductive, so when leading conference calls, strive to keep everyone on point. If someone asks an off-topic question, politely offer to address it offline, where it can receive due attention. When a critical decision needs to be made, make sure you have asked everyone for their input. Finally, to ensure team alignment on the topic, do not end the call without going around the virtual room to get a confirmation of understanding from everyone.

Yes, having multiple people on a call can be challenging, and that is what makes videoconferencing such a good option. It allows you to share your computer screen (or phone screen) with others and use visuals to hold a participant's attention and work more productively. I like using Zoom videoconferencing because it is easy to use, mobile friendly, and offers screen sharing.

HELPFUL TIPS

Whether you find yourself teleconferencing or videoconferencing with your team, check out the following tips to get the most out of your meetings:

- Send out the meeting agenda well ahead of time.

- Set a time limit for the call and let participants know what it is. As the moderator, make sure to call in early and start the meeting on time. Do not wait for stragglers.

- Keep your own statements brief, pause often to ask others for their feedback, and confirm that everyone is clear on what is being discussed.

- Encourage everyone to present their point of view on the problem (including individuals who have remained silent).

- Do not let anyone leave the call without knowing that they understand the decisions and next steps, if applicable.

The following ground rules should apply to everyone:

- If you are on a cell phone, make sure that you are in a quiet spot and have a strong signal and charged battery.

- Be present. Have someone else handle distractions, so that you can provide your undivided attention during the call.

- Keep statements and questions relevant to the agenda or issue at hand.

The Perils of Micromanagement

The world of healthcare is fast moving with never a dull moment, and caring for patients is complex, unpredictable work. As leaders of a project team, we all have patient care responsibilities, so who has the time to micromanage? Believe it or not, there are plenty of project managers who fall into the trap of over-control. Are you one of them?

Understanding the need for control raises a "chicken-egg" causality dilemma. Do the duties and responsibilities of managing a project force people to become "control freaks" or do people who need to exert control gravitate toward project management? In my experience, and with all due respect, I think many project managers are by nature control freaks, myself included. But how can we blame ourselves when the buck stops with us?

Although the breadth of responsibility that project managers must shoulder can be unfair, it is sometimes better to step back from seeking complete control and trust your *Healthy Team*. Remember that managing a PCE project is not about you, but about the team that you are leading. Your task is to guide a project, share what you know, and determine what your team members need to accomplish their tasks on any given day. The last thing you need to do, or should want to do, is stand in front of people all day telling them what to do instead of allowing them to think on their own. You must put controls in place, set up the necessary project tools and templates, and clearly communicate pertinent information. Not only will this promote a productive workflow, it will show your team members that you trust their abilities and value their contributions. On the personal side, it will help you sleep better at night and avoid professional burnout.

TRUST INSTITUTIONAL MAVENS

I have found that some of the best "get it done" people on the hospital staff are OR and emergency room (ER) personnel. These professionals understand what needs to be done and accept the responsibility of being on a project team. Rethink your efforts to micromanage these folks. You might well wind up having to deal with a less-than-pleased head nurse, for example, which is not the best situation.

On one of my OR projects, a nurse named Bob dutifully attended every meeting and was very involved with providing the team with good input and operational ideas. At each meeting, I would ask him if a task was finished or if something was ready. Eventually, he started giving me the eye and responding, "Are you really asking me that? Of course, Cathy. That was done the day after we talked about it." After working with him for a while, I began to view the situation in a different light, wondering if his response was perhaps due to how often I was "on him," or the way in which I asked for updates. But I trusted Bob, so I let go of the reins a bit. After all, it felt good to know that he could take care of his responsibilities and leave me with one less worry on my plate.

Of course, I continued to ask him for project updates, but I made sure he knew that I knew his work would be completed as promised. I kept things light, joking that he should think of me as being a "human database" collecting information and keeping records up to date. He would chuckle at this, marking a welcome shift in how we interacted from then on.

ER projects can be particularly challenging because many department functions are associated with outside entities—EMS, police and fire departments, and community shelters—about which a team might not be fully knowledgeable. The head nurse also plays a powerful role here, proficiently running the ER like a maestro leading an orchestra, and it is best to collaborate closely with this person.

I learned this the hard way during a project meeting when our team discussed closing down different areas of the ER over a six-week period. I had suggested ways to partition off and protect one of the hallways, not knowing that the head nurse had already run her own plan by the superintendent. She presented her plan as an "FYI" item. Based on her response to suggestions I made to her plan, it was clear that I needed to let her take the lead.

Was it a good idea to let the head nurse take over project logistics? Yes and no. The answer depends on the individual and circumstances involved. In this scenario, yes, because she had done a great job in planning out the closure, and so it was best to not micromanage the task. But in another situation, or with another hospital staff member, the answer might be no. The person wanting to lead the effort might lack the necessary experience or knowledge to do so. You might also encounter a staff member who will not fully cooperate because they want to protect their "turf." These scenarios can cause scheduling delays and increase project costs.

If you do let someone take over a task that you generally run, make sure the plan is feasible and you are kept in the loop. The head nurse and I shared a mutual respect for each other. As far as I was concerned, she had earned her stripes with her experience and solid, executable plan. And she respected me by keeping me informed.

In closing, it is important that you remain open to delegating tasks and giving people breathing room to complete them. You might have to jump in from time to time, but if your project is well structured with clear rules from the outset (you have a *Healthy Project*), and if the team is communicating together well (you have a *Healthy Team*), then everyone will work efficiently within established parameters. So try not to be an unrelenting taskmaster. In fact, have some fun and enjoy spending time with your team. Think of yourself as a reformed control freak, and you will be surprised at how you can be both professionally and personally enriched by resisting the urge to micromanage the process.

Situations Out of Your Control

You plan, you forecast, and you listen to your team members. Despite your best intentions, things will happen that are completely out of your control. How you handle unforeseen situations can make or break your reputation. Your initial, natural reaction might be to dive in and try to fix the situation. Or you might choose to do nothing and see what happens. Either way, things can still spin out of control, as in the following renovation story.

It was the day of the ribbon-cutting ceremony for a renovated children's area in a hospital ER. All the requisite dignitaries, including the mayor, were in attendance, and the hospital president was set to give a speech. The showpiece of the new space was a large aquarium. Earlier in the day, however, the department director had decided that there were not enough vibrantly colored fish in the tank to impress the crowd, and so she asked a staff member, Mike, to purchase more fish to augment the existing population.

Mike, who had no experience with aquarium fish, headed out to the pet store and picked out a beautiful, long purple fish, along with several other pastel-colored fish. The celebration was set for the afternoon, so he suspended the bagged fish in the tank for a few hours to allow the fish to acclimate to the tank water. Fifteen minutes before the start of the event, Mike released the new fish into the tank. There to greet them was a large grouper that took an immediate liking to the purple fish.

The next thing I knew I was on the phone with Mike, who was panic-stricken. I hurried to the ER children's area, where I found him standing on a chair and bent over the tank, trying desperately to separate the fish with a net. I stood with my mouth open in shock, but quickly realized that there was no way to stop Mother Nature. All I could do was convince three team members to stand in front of the aquarium throughout the ceremony to block any view of the fish feast, which lasted nearly an hour.

When projects go awry, you must be nimble enough to deal with factors that fall outside of your control. First assess the situation. Then either dive in to resolve it or stand back and let it play itself out. Always remain calm because the nature of running PCE projects means there will be plenty of unknowns hiding in your plans and more than enough people above your pay grade who will make decisions that affect your project in unexpected ways.

ADMINISTRATIVE ROADBLOCKS

Healthcare provider partnerships and mergers can be time consuming and complex with many layers of red tape. Although C-suite executives are getting smarter about how to forge institutional relationships, working out the kinks can take time.

In one case, our project scope was to build an urgent care center in a neighboring town. The hospital had partnered with a company specializing in managing urgent care centers, an emerging competitive market. It offered the hospital a turn-key operation that included the design and build of the center, its opening, and the ongoing management of the back office and staff.

Since the company was headquartered in Florida, the administration approved our request to manage the project design and build phases. We wanted this responsibility because working long distance was not the firm's greatest strength and it was not familiar with the local healthcare market or department of building regulations. We had also witnessed issues arise during the firm's negotiation of the center's lease.

A few months into the project, the hospital unexpectedly decided to partner with a different company. By then our team had arrived at an innovative design that promised to set the hospital apart from its competition and allow it to tap into a new market. Already on track with a timely move-in date, we now had to work with a new partner that was not up to speed with the new deal. Unfortunately, questions about equipment specifications and the timing of staff hiring, among other issues, wound up delaying our schedule and kept us from opening the center on time.

To bounce back from our dilemma, we relied on our flexibility and good team communication. Two team members served as liaisons and took the wheel in soliciting direction from the new company. Meanwhile, the rest of the us collaborated on completing the construction. The entire team met weekly to recalibrate dates and expectations, and I distributed meeting minutes to keep everyone informed and on task.

Being unable to move forward on a project for reasons outside your control can be very frustrating and discouraging for you and your team. Although the hospital was technically responsible for delaying the center's completion and grand opening, as project manager, I had to take the best steps possible under the circumstances. Rather than leave everything on hold while waiting for answers, I quickly maneuvered around the restrictions to get us to where we needed to be, all thanks to my committed team.

You might wonder then why you should worry about a project delay if the healthcare system or a decision maker at the top is responsible for it. Never assume that you will not be held accountable, so keep accurate records and communicate often with everyone involved. If you find yourself holding the hot potato of blame, your meticulous documentation—including e-mails and text messages—will prove invaluable for recreating a timeline of discussions and events. I cannot tell you how many times I have had to provide a blow-by-blow account. Reports can be lifesavers. (*See* Resources, page 297.)

 HELPFUL TIPS

There are a few more things to remember if you wind up having to work with a new partner or vendor midstream in a project:

[1]   **Establish and maintain contact.** Meet with the new participants as soon as possible to identify their priorities and bring them up to speed on the project, including its history and any challenges. Keep them in the loop as much as you can.

[2] **Do not forgo status reports.** Monthly status reports should be part of any project process, but when a situation arises that is out of your control, they are especially useful. Make sure that you chronicle in detail the work performed to date, highlighting pending decisions, necessary action steps, the reasons for any problems or delays, and any other information that will keep the C-suite confident that everything is being handled well.

[3] **Follow the money.** Always know from which cost center your budget money is originating. If a new partner joins the project, the cost center could change, which could cause delays, such as with equipment purchasing.

CHANGE ORDERS

I hate change orders because they take up too much of everyone's time, generate loads of paperwork, and disrupt budgets and schedules. Change orders can often come from the top. For example, management might want the project completed within an unrealistic timeframe that remains uncontested by a project manager.

The reality is that an approved schedule does not necessarily reflect the actual time needed for a design team to develop a highly detailed set of plans that will allow a contractor to comprehensively price out the work. In a one-two punch, the schedule will not only slip, it can become seriously compromised if important plan details go missing, leading to a constant flow of unexpected change orders.

Add to these change orders any additional ones that can come if your engineer or architect has missed any preexisting mechanical conflicts that should have been identified prior to the planning and design phases. (This is why I appreciate it when engineers who I interview show up with a ladder and a flashlight instead of in a suit and tie. It tells me that they are serious about collecting the right information for my project.)

 ## HELPFUL TIPS

When change orders creep into your project, they will take considerable time to review, get approved, and subsequently manage, causing work to come to a screeching halt and potentially putting you over budget. You can lessen or avoid any negative consequences through good planning at the outset. Remember to:

[1] **Share information.** It is worth repeating that you should encourage your team members to fully share their insights and knowledge, especially on such matters as specialty equipment, technology, procedures, and finishes, to name but a few.

[2] **Anticipate change orders.** Have a policy in place at the project's start for how change orders are managed. You do not want to be distracted by red tape if you have to put out a project fire.

[3] **Negotiate!** Do not let a contractor begin work without knowing exactly what the rate will be for any change orders, as well as for any other important details.

I always say, "If you do not plan accordingly in the beginning, get ready to pay in the end," which naturally leads us to the next uncontrollable scenario.

INHERITING BAD DECISIONS

Some hospitals are averse to discarding old equipment, which can cause problems for your team. Unfortunately, you might not have the authority to do anything about it. My team and I were once tasked with renovating a pharmacy clean room and bringing it up to standard. It had a 20-year-old pharmaceutical mixing hood (used when handling and compounding drugs). Although we were budgeted for two new hoods, the department director did not want to discard the old hood and made this known to the VP of nursing, who asked the purchasing department to sell it. Unfortunately, no buyer could be found, and so the hood bounced around the hospital.

By phase one of construction, there was still no plan for the old hood. By then I considered myself released from being responsible for the equipment. I was wrong. We had to move the hood out of the construction area, and it ended up on the loading dock. A month later, the loading dock manager asked me to remove the hood because it smelled and he lacked the room to store it.

Once again, the VP of nursing stepped in and decided that the hood could be used in phase two of construction. It would be installed in the pharmacy's temporary location, but not right away, so I hired both a mover to transfer the hood to an unused storage space and another company to clean it. A few months later, I needed to measure the hood prior to its move to the pharmacy's temporary space only to discover that the facilities guys had discarded the hood after being told to clean out the storage space. All I could do was laugh at the irony. We could have saved so much time and money had we simply disposed of the hood from the get-go. The lesson here is that although many decisions are made and handed to us, it is our job to guide a project to a successful completion.

PLAIN OLD LADY LUCK

Even if you have managed your project to the best of your ability and everyone is on the same page, unforeseen developments can take the wind out of your sails. There is one such project that I will never forget.

Hospital systems have been "buying up" physician groups at a rapid clip to expand their provider networks. The terms of such office mergers might not always be clearly communicated to a project team. Unfortunately, there is no cookie-cutter approach to dealing with them. In my experience, how you run this type of project will all come down to the type of deal struck between the parties involved.

The hospital in this story had just purchased a primary care physician practice. Our mission was to reconstruct the practice's existing offices, which had not been renovated in three decades. The work required moving the practice to a temporary space for four months. Meanwhile, the hospital would assume the lease for the physician-owned suite of offices that was in a building owned by a condo association.

Our team completed the construction plans for an efficient new space, and everyone happily approved them. But just after the practice was relocated, and before construction began, an under-sink water heater broke, causing water to flood the back offices of the L-shaped space and the garage area. A few days later our team, along with the insurance carrier, assessed the damage through some testing and discovered mold. We remediated the space within two weeks of the flood event, but we were then pressured to immediately begin construction.

Since the front offices did not appear to have suffered any flood damage, I approved the start of the demolition in that area to get the schedule back on track. However, knowing that mold can quickly spread, I recommended to my boss that we also test the offices at both the front and rear of the space. The results indicated the presence of mold, and we again had to perform remediation.

We began questioning how the mold in the front area of the suite could have occurred. The back area of the suite, which had flooded, was tented. Had the tenting been compromised? Did the mold remediation company not do a thorough job? We were dogged by this uncertainty for several weeks.

Remediation work is not cheap, and it can throw off your budget by tens of thousands of dollars and delay your schedule by several weeks. Unfortunately, the hospital had to pick up the bill because the practice's insurance did not cover the service.

Needless to say, our weekly project meetings were not fun. The team had to repeatedly report that work could not move forward due to the unknown cause of the additional mold. The physicians blamed me because my construction crew could not begin work on the same day that the practice had moved out. They also believed that if the construction crew had been working when the water heater burst, the problem could have been addressed immediately.

Hospital politics at the top put pressure on my boss, who asked me to hire an external project manager while I managed the project "behind the scenes." After a longer, more extensive investigation, we were shocked to find that the mold had been present throughout the building's exterior stucco walls for many years and was unrelated to the flood. But we were also dismayed over the extended delay that would be caused by a full remediation. I had to come to the table as the bearer of bad news—that since the mold problem was a preexisting issue, further remediation would be the condo association's responsibility.

After we handed off the testing and remediation to the association, we staunched the hemorrhaging of project costs. By then, however, our schedule had become greatly extended. It took more than eight months to hold all the necessary homeowner meetings and for the association to raise the capital for the remediation. Picking up the pieces of a project on hold for a year had its challenges, including dealing with the increased costs of delay claims and of storing furniture and other items. Fortunately, the practice had continued seeing patients in its temporary space.

As grueling as the experience was, we as a team were highly responsive in getting the project back up and running, and I credit my team members for their hard work and persistence. Tackling such a sticky situation had required us to quickly identify all the challenges and establish responsibility for addressing them, while not succumbing to the drama even if things got brutal, which they did. The head physician had taken out his frustration on all of us. Although his emotional reaction was not entirely surprising, given the impact of the project delays on his business, staff, and patients, it was nevertheless an unproductive stance for seeking a resolution. I was called incompetent, a liar, and the physicians had requested that I be taken off the project. I became a target despite the fact that the project had been well planned out and the physicians themselves were very involved in the construction planning and team meetings.

Contributing to the confusion was the added complexity of a merger involving a physician practice made up of tenant-owners. Back then, such mergers represented uncharted waters. One could argue that the true source of our strife was the original purchasing agreement drawn up between the hospital and the practice. The understandable desire for a quick and successful merger might not have allowed for a full vetting of the real-estate portion of the deal and the inclusion of a clause in the agreement that would cover mishaps.

If your project is crushed under the heel of Lady Luck, exercise both patience and tenacity because it can take time for things to iron themselves out. Proactively and thoroughly review contractual agreements. Never be afraid to speak up and do the right thing for your client. Fortunately, I had experience with leasing deals, contracts, and mold remediation, and so I understood what was happening and how political the situation had become.

Finally, keep to the facts. I kept pushing forward armed with documentation, which paid off once the CFO stepped in because the mold problem had become costly. Filling in the upper management, lawyers, and real-estate professionals on all the details allowed them to make informed decisions regarding a new lease, which ultimately included mold-testing requirements to protect the patients, staff, and hospital in the future.

PARTING ADVICE

When problems arise at any point during initiation, planning, execution, monitoring, and close out—be they the result of an internal mix-up or external circumstances—remember that you can manage your way through them expeditiously, effectively, and with controlled fallout by adhering to the following three overarching rules for managing a project's rough patches.

Confront Reality Head On

First, sometimes we need to play detective and look at the project's big picture. In the mold remediation story, the problem was not a straightforward one. There were many layers and challenges to it that involved the merger deal itself, hospital politics, and the emotional reality of having one's business bought out by a large corporation. No one had expected the mold complication and we had to navigate through uncharted territory.

Second, your best defense is a good controls offense. Think of meeting minutes, monthly status reports, and budgets as being part of an overarching alert system for your project management. For example, monthly status reports put critical information in front of administrators, who expect to hear about the progress of the project, the budget, the schedule, decisions to be made, and any "people issues" affecting the project's momentum. Compiling a report involves distilling a lot of information into essential points that impart clarity to a project. Is your budget on target? Do you need to change course in some way before moving forward? Is there a potential roadblock up ahead? (*See* Resources, page 297, for more on project controls.)

Third, communicate, communicate! Tackle even tough-to-discuss matters head on and as soon as possible before they become major headaches. Above all, never cover up problems, but instead bring them out into the light and offer solutions for them.

KEEP CALM AND MANAGE ON

When I started as a project management consultant, my first boss, Ray Quartararo, would not only tell me to stay calm during tough situations, but to be the calmest person on the team. As I look back on my years of running many projects, this is one of the best pieces of advice that I can pass along. When everything is coming at you in what feels like an overwhelming torrent, stand back and collect yourself (literally take a breath, relax your body, and focus). If you open yourself up to this state of being, you will find calmness to be your greatest virtue as a project manager during stressful times. You will be able to clearly and honestly assess the challenges of a situation, communicate effectively with all parties, wield the facts with powerful persuasion, and be prepared in general.

For example, early on I will ask my team to talk about what they think might go wrong as well as right throughout the project process. We would then cover all the project areas, including budget management, C-suite expectations, the realities of designing a PCE, keeping up on status updates, contingency planning, and routine relationship building. We would also come up with strategies for each project topic. Just the exercise alone of planning for any undesired events will help you and your team remain calm if anything does happen.

Conclusion

When a project takes an unexpected turn or if you are in doubt regarding a matter, simply revisit the underlying principles of *Health Well Done: Healthy Patient, Healthy Team,* and *Healthy Project.* Are you focused on the principles of *Healthy Patient?* Talk with your team to return to and reaffirm the primary reason behind why you are all working together in the first place. Remind each other that all the time, money, and sweat spent are for an important goal. Others are counting on you to successfully create an environment in which patients can feel safe, cared for, and able to achieve a state of wellness, and that it could well be you sitting in the patient chair.

Are you respecting the importance of a *Healthy Team?* Make sure that you have the right people, and the right number of people, on board to share wisdom and experience and apply that wealth of knowledge to the decision-making process. Renew the team members' trust and confidence in themselves and each other. Revisit your project vision and scope. Are they still aligned with your end goal?

To get back on track with a *Healthy Project,* test the soundness of the project's structure through productive weekly meetings and detailed, up-to-date, and—most important of all—realistic budgets and schedules. Root out problems early on and decisively and quickly eliminate their causes. Step back to ascertain whether a problem is within your control, all the while working through the situation in the best way you can.

Above all, do not stick your head in the sand hoping that the problem will just resolve on its own or simply go away. Stay connected to your team and keep an eagle eye on every step of the process.

⚬━ KEY TAKEAWAYS

As a team leader, you are only as good as the strength of your team.

Projects maintain their forward momentum with timely decision making.

Change is good as long as its value is communicated to the end user. Make a good case for change and reinforce it often. "Before and after" visual aids can help stakeholders imagine the final space.

Involve everyone in creating the project schedule, and give it a reality check by confirming actual timelines and gauging the potential impact of the schedule on project tasks.

Recognize that people are often distracted, so reach out often and go beyond memos and e-mails. Try texting, storytelling, and even using (appropriate) humor.

Remember that the buck always stops with you.

Accept that you cannot control everything. Step back and trust your *Healthy Team*.

Make the most of your institutional mavens. Follow their lead and let them do their job.

If you do not plan accordingly in the beginning, get ready to pay at the end of the project.

THE FUTURE OF
HEALTH WELL DONE

6

"When we try to pick out anything by itself, we find it hitched to everything else in the Universe."

– John Muir

You can commit to becoming the best possible project manager, assemble the greatest team, and plan the most well-coordinated project, but no matter how diligently you work to build an outstanding patient-centered healthcare environment (PCE) and regardless of the many successes under your belt, you will face growing demands to provide high-quality results.

Practicing the best project leadership means meeting challenges and leveraging opportunities and, above all, staying on top of an industry in perpetual flux. This final chapter explores the ways in which your PCE projects might be affected as the nation's healthcare industry continues to transform. It provides insights into how you can succeed by continuing to rely on the principles of the *Health Well Done* approach, and it ends with an important reminder of how our collective state of wellness is inextricably linked to the health and well-being of the planet itself.

About Population Health

Before examining the ongoing evolution of healthcare delivery, it is worth touching on the concept of population health. A relatively new term, population health lacks a uniform definition. It can refer to the health of a community or a specific population of individuals, such as defined by geography, demographics, or clinical diagnoses. Or it might refer to the goal of taking care of the greatest number of people at the lowest cost. In their article, "What Is Population Health?" David Kindig and Greg Stoddart define population health as "the health outcome of a group of individuals, including the distribution of such outcomes within the group," and that the field "includes health outcomes, patterns of health determinants, and policies and interventions that link these two."[1]

To these definitions of population health, I would add my own expanded version, which is that population health concerns the general populations of all living things—humans, animals, plants, bacteria—and of the earth itself. Just as our planet is healthy when its flora and fauna are healthy, so too are we humans healthy as a species when our collective mental, physical, and spiritual states are healthy.

Understanding the relevance of population health to planning and executing a PCE project is important for project management because as hospitals transition from a fee-for-service model to a fee-for-value model (with built-in pay-for-performance incentives), they will be graded and paid on patient outcomes and keeping patients well. Remember that patients are consumers and, according to Nielsen, most consumers consider recommendations from family and friends to be the most credible form of advertising.[2] Designing healthcare environments that keep patients loyal and referring other patients to a healthcare system is naturally a C-suite's priority, which makes it a concern for a project manager. If the PCE you build does not fulfill consumer needs, other healthcare systems or companies will be happy to step in.

COMPETING IN THE HEALTHCARE MARKETPLACE

Population health research, leveraged effectively, can help a healthcare system compete in the marketplace by informing its efforts to monitor outcomes, improve the coordination of care, and identify and address gaps in care. Population health research is heavily driven by quantitative data and their analysis, but this raw data cannot tell the whole story about the needs of patients and medical professionals in the built environment. Project teams need to hear directly from the front-line caregivers, as well as abide by real-time local and global health-related events and developments that will affect hospital systems and their patient populations. In other words, it is not enough to measure health outcomes. Hard data must go hand in hand with the indispensable qualitative work that healthcare professionals perform, and which provides the context necessary for distilling a story out of numbers. And therein lies the challenge. How are healthcare systems interpreting and applying good data and how well are their healthcare models keeping up?

The reality is that although healthcare systems have opportunities to make significant and positive differences in health outcomes, they can be stymied by the overwhelmingly vast quantity of big data available and unable to translate the information into actionable strategies that move the needle on quality and cost. The good news is that organizations are recognizing the value of evidence-based design by examining case studies that show viable ways to provide seamless, coordinated, and cost-effective patient-centered care. Three case studies of note are described in project briefs by The Center for Health Design (CHD) and involve Adelante Healthcare in Mesa, Arizona, the Clinica Family Health People's Medical Clinic in Boulder, Colorado, and the Kaiser Permanente Antelope Valley Medical Offices in Lancaster, California.

Adelante Healthcare Mesa, a nonprofit center that serves low-income, uninsured, and underinsured populations, promotes healthy living through its "high work efficiency environment." Its adherence to evidence-based design relies on a patient-centered medical home (PCMH) model—holistic and coordinated team-based primary care—to support its population health goals. This includes improved patient access and flow and the delivery of an optimal patient experience, achieved through "talking room design, pod design, decentralized team work spaces, geographical location and co-location of services, and healing environment elements."[3]

The PCMH is also the model of care at the People's Medical Clinic, a successful Clinica Family Health facility certified by the National Committee for Quality Assurance. It uses population health data to support the qualitative work being done to benefit a low-income, underinsured population, with efforts centered on optimizing patient access to care, care quality, and care safety. "The common function among each design concept (from pod design to team collaboration spaces to group visit rooms) can be simply stated as 'bringing people together.'"[4]

Maximizing direct patient involvement is also an important goal in population health. Gigi DeSouki, founder and CEO of Wellness on Wheels, Inc., connects population health with the "individual responsibility for physical, mental, spiritual and social health. When each person takes control of his or her health, it reflects on our families and society as a whole."[5] Few people would disagree that healthcare systems can be greatly supportive in this respect. In the CHD's case study of the Antelope Valley Medical Offices, which serves a community with many patients who are chronically ill, project design is driven by the goals of engaging the community and promoting health and wellness.[6] The facility's design reflects a strong focus on sustainability (it is LEED platinum certified) and the community's need for specialty services to treat obesity, diabetes, and cancer.

Regardless of how population health is used to improve healthcare delivery, the consensus is that project managers must continually explore new ways to optimize the healthcare setting and promote the concept of collective health and wellness, keeping in mind that the C-suite will always be looking for ways to leverage a project's design to get more without paying more. And be warned that you might be given a project scope without knowing the basis for the top-level decisions made. Stay open-minded, but arm yourself with population health information that applies to your specific healthcare system. It will keep your team's frustration levels low and help you better serve the community.

The Shifting Healthcare Landscape

To understand what the future might hold for us in our everyday work as project managers of PCEs, or in the context of the *Health Well Done* framework, it helps to briefly examine current trends in the healthcare industry. As we all know, healthcare is big business—and will likely remain so—and the primary challenge for those in the business is to be profitable while creating a caring patient and family experience that fosters loyalty to the healthcare system's brand. This tricky balancing act must be achieved in the face of legislative unpredictability, new (and sometimes disruptive) technologies, and growing patient expectations in the type and quality of healthcare received.

A major factor affecting the patient care choices being made by healthcare systems is the ongoing transition of points of care from hospitals to people's homes and other locations, where technology determines the scope, level, and convenience of services offered. Fierce competition exists for market share. What follows are several categories of concern—and promise— that project managers should pay close attention to as the delivery of healthcare continues to adapt to changing winds.

THE IMPACT OF HEALTHCARE LEGISLATION

Healthcare is a politically and emotionally charged topic with complex challenges and opposing sides. Historically, politics has had a major impact on healthcare facility design. In 1945, President Harry Truman presented to Congress a five-part program for improving the health and availability of healthcare for Americans. In answer to his first proposal, Congress passed the

Hospital Survey and Construction (Hill–Burton) Act in 1946, which provided loans and grants to health facilities, including hospitals and nursing homes, for construction and modernization. In return, facilities were to provide a certain volume of free and reduced-cost care to their local communities. Although funding coming from the program was halted in 1997, a number of healthcare facilities are still obligated to provide services under the act.

The 2010 passage of the Patient Protection and Affordable Care Act (ACA) under President Barack Obama revolutionized the health insurance industry by: insuring a large number of Americans, including more young adults; mandating coverage for preexisting conditions and preventive care; expanding Medicaid; limiting health insurance company profits; removing lifetime benefit limits; offering protection from policy cancellations; and strengthening patient-appeal rights. But there has been fallout worth noting. In an interview by *The Sun*, Andrew Coates, founder of Single Payer New York and past president of Physicians for a National Health Program, points out how the ACA has "led to an enormous wave of corporate conglomeration—among hospitals, primary care networks, insurance companies, and pharmacies—creating huge new entities, all in the search for profit and market share."[7]

Nevertheless, with provisions in place to reduce the number of uninsured Americans, healthcare systems have gone from being "fixers" to "preventers" of illness. To meet the needs of the increased population of insured patients, ambulatory care facilities, imaging centers, and walk-in clinics began appearing in local neighborhoods (including in such venues as Walgreens, CVS, and Target), siphoning off revenues from traditional hospitals. Hospitals, in turn, have been adjusting to the new competition by investing more in outpatient facilities.

Many changes have taken place and the healthcare landscape remains uncertain from a legislative standpoint. Strong support for the dismantling of the ACA from President Donald Trump and many members of Congress has already led to the elimination of the individual mandate and might result in future reforms to Medicare and Medicaid. The political winds will continue to shift and have an impact on the design of healthcare facilities. The only sure bet is the unabating demand by patients to become educated on their health and healthcare and to receive high-quality patient care, whether it happens in hospitals, in their neighborhoods, or at home.

So how do we turn away from what some might view as a "de-evolution" of healthcare delivery to create a model that more closely reflects the better part of our social natures? Coates, who is also an assistant professor of medicine and psychiatry at Albany Medical College, believes that the "care of human beings should not be a commodity. Since the dawn of time people have done their best to tend to the injured or sick. That's something very basic to humanity."[8] In other words, as a nation, we need to determine whether we will take responsibility for our citizenry or leave people to their own devices in the absence of a decision and as the healthcare battle rages on in the halls of government.

NEW POINTS OF SERVICE

Healthcare systems and companies are putting ever-greater responsibility on the shoulders of patients through procedures and drug packaging tailored to individuals. This comes in response to a rise in patients being released from the hospital while still needing services. Two resulting healthcare trends to close the gap of care, and which should be on every project manager's radar, are the evolution of the home-based care market and the rise of distribution centers for drugs and medical equipment. Telehealth technologies have been emerging that support adherence to ongoing treatment by, for example, communicating information back to providers and by facilitating self-care and providing patient education. Other developments include the use of GPS technology by medical professionals for home or workplace visits, as well as mobile services, such as vans equipped with specialized medical equipment to deliver offsite treatment. But even the need itself for in-person visits has begun to decrease, thanks to smartphone apps that can pair with wearable monitors to record blood pressure level, sugar level, and heart rate, and transmit the data back to providers.

Technology is also changing the belief that patient care must be conventional. The trend now is to create value by reducing costs and building care into everyday life to keep things simple and allow patients more freedom. Big Pharma is getting into the game of accommodating patient lifestyles by tailoring their products in ways that support treatment adherence. For example, a company might market a psoriasis ointment that is unscented, easy to apply, and sleekly packaged to an active 17-year-old girl who, typically, might be worried about her appearance. A 70-year-old man requiring dialysis can still enjoy vacation cruises by taking advantage of a service called Dialysis at Sea. Companies might offer private one-day comprehensive testing that fits into the schedules of their busy executives.

The rise of convenience services that accommodate patient preferences and lifestyles means that "traditional" hospitals will increasingly become service points for the very sick while outpatient service providers of routine and preventive care services grow their businesses. PCE project managers are well served by keeping abreast of this important shift in the delivery of care because any one of the countless new ideas being explored and tested might one day appear in blueprints and budgets.

TECHNOLOGY AND WORKFLOW

I once had to escort my mother to a surgical ambulatory center for a procedure. As we sat in the waiting room, a kind-looking man appeared with an iPad that displayed real-time information about the appointment. He told us that in 10 minutes we would be alerted (by beeper) to head for the pre-op room, and that surgery would take place 30 minutes later and last 90 minutes.

This coupling of technology and workflow process is an example of applying *Health Well Done* concepts to improving operations and, in turn, patient care. And why not? Big businesses leverage their technological capabilities to make the shopping experience more convenient and efficient. Companies like UPS and Amazon allow consumers to track their delivery workflow. Healthcare systems are waking up to the fact that communication, transparency, and efficient information delivery can reduce stress and anxiety for patients and their families.

Builders of PCEs should never stop investigating how to best incorporate these and other innovations into their efforts to improve the delivery of care or to stop talking to PCE end users about their preferred medical technologies and techniques and how they affect physical environments. For example, a hospital could decide to implement a new electronic medical records system, such as Epic, to make it easier and more efficient for its physicians and other clinical staff to deliver outstanding patient care.

The resulting changes to scheduling, billing, and the revenue cycle, along with analytic capabilities, could trigger new projects. Additional offices might need to be created to accommodate the personnel hired to assume any new job titles created by the implementation. The transition to a new system might also affect the patient experience and clinical workflow. For example, you might need to build a patient kiosk in a lobby or install more wireless access points (WAPs) for network connectivity.

Make sure that you know why you are altering operations and how any changes will affect the delivery of patient care. Any changes or improvements made to space, equipment, or protocol will still need to satisfy patient safety and cost concerns. You can maximize your efforts by keeping up with trends and the politics of healthcare. This can be done by keeping an eye on Wall Street and industry movers and shakers, attending conferences such as those held by ASHE, IHI, Planetree, and the CHD, and setting up Google alerts for "future trends in healthcare," "healthcare innovations," and other search topics.

"People-Oriented" Challenges

Although progress is being made in meeting patients where they are and in incorporating beneficial technologies for patients and staff alike, there remain two "people-oriented" challenges that must not be abdicated by hospital systems: the "compromised patient experience" and the rise of occupational stress and burnout among medical professionals.

HEALTHCARE SHOULD HELP, NOT HURT

As I talked about in Chapter 1, more people than ever are educating themselves about wellness and researching the good, the bad, and the ugly of healthcare providers. Personal stories abound on the challenges of navigating the U.S. healthcare system, most frequently on social media platforms, where negative stories appear to far outweigh positive ones. One story that I find useful to share is about my grad school colleague Germaine (from Chapter 1), a plucky nurse who once found herself, as she describes, "one hospitalization away from bankruptcy."

Following an overseas trip involving dozens of hours of flying across multiple days, Germaine began suffering from considerable shortness of breath upon minimal exertion. The doctor's office could not fit her in for an appointment on the same day she called to describe her symptoms, but that evening a partner called her back, concerned about her potentially serious condition. He and Germaine both suspected pulmonary emboli, and he advised her to immediately head for the emergency department. A self-described "stubborn, know-it-all healthcare practitioner," Germaine firmly declined and said that she would see him in the morning.

The next day she was seen by the physician and was immediately admitted into the hospital, where she spent 18 hours undergoing numerous tests and procedures, at an ultimate out-of-pocket cost of thousands of dollars. Although her experience with the physician was initially very positive, this veteran hospital nurse found herself fighting other healthcare professionals regarding interventions that she felt were repetitive or unnecessary. Although this is understandable, Germaine surely also understood that the medical professionals treating her were doing what they believed was necessary to provide her with the highest quality care. Fortunately, Germaine recovered, although at a cost she felt was exorbitant.

Germaine's experiences echo those of countless patients who seek the optimal healthcare system experience, yet might also find themselves facing potentially enormous financial costs, often unbeknownst to many providers who are trying to deliver the highest quality of care while facing their own professional pressures to control costs or limit potential liability. Added to this stress are the personal pressures they face and their potential for becoming another statistic in the epidemic of professional burnout.

PHYSICIAN AND STAFF BURNOUT

Ever-changing compliance, government, and insurance requirements have exacerbated the already tremendous burden put on physicians, nurses, and other medical staff, and have specifically led to high rates of physician burnout. According to Tait D. Shanafelt and John H. Noseworthy of the Mayo Clinic, "National studies suggest that at least 50 percent of U.S. physicians are experiencing professional burnout."[9] Burnout can have serious personal and professional consequences. In terms of patient well-being, physician burnout can lead to "decreased quality of care and increased medical errors, decreased patient satisfaction, decreased productivity and professional effort, and physician turnover." Personal repercussions include "broken relationships, alcohol and substance use, depression, and suicide."[10]

To address the issue, hospital systems are examining evidence-based practices to prevent unnecessary occupational suffering.

However, some critics warn against putting the burden on professionals. Rather, as Shanafelt and Noseworthy point out, "Extensive evidence suggests that the organization and practice environment play critical roles in whether physicians remain engaged or burn out."[11]

A nurse once told me that her supervisor would post memos inside bathroom stalls to force nurses to read them, illustrating how difficult it is for nurses catch a break. Clearly, healthcare systems should provide comprehensive resources to address mounting pressures on medical staff. Their priority should be creating optimal healthcare settings that reduce staff stress, increase physician engagement, and improve job satisfaction to help professionals remain true to why they entered the medical field in the first place—to help people. A hospital's culture should reflect a philosophy of caring for the caregiver by supporting PCE amenities that foster staff well-being, including ample natural light, massage chairs, and areas and opportunities for rest and refuge, such as a meditation room that can double as a place to hold a yoga class.

By keeping these considerations at the forefront of your project planning and execution, you will uphold the principles of *Healthy Patient*, since physicians, nurses, and other hospital staff play important roles on a *Healthy Team*. The better you understand their workflow and patient care needs, the better your PCE will support healthy, productive patient-provider relationships.

Resources You Can Turn To

Despite the many complex concerns and challenges facing the U.S. healthcare industry, areas of consensus do exist regarding the delivery of care. The Facility Guidelines Institute (FGI) is an independent, nonprofit organization that oversees the publication and periodic revision of three central documents: the *FGI Guidelines for Design and Construction* for hospitals; for outpatient facilities; and for residential health, care, and support facilities. Developed in partnership with other healthcare industry groups, these invaluable resources offer evidence-based support, including minimum design standards, and they are relied upon by healthcare organizations, design firms, and state and federal agencies.

Yet productive consensus can be undermined by media influence. Pundits tout their superior brands of healthcare policy on political talk shows and Twitter feeds, making it no surprise that many everyday Americans are feeling a sense of doom and gloom about the nation's healthcare system. Cutting through the onslaught of negative headlines and making meaningful progress is not impossible, but it does require a groundswell of real commitment and unity by physicians, hospitals, healthcare administrators and executives, and legislators to partner with the modern-day patient-consumer. Decision makers from the halls of Congress to C-suite conference rooms must roll up their sleeves and solve problems through patience, determination, thoroughness, and unbiased pragmatism.

How can you deliver on your commitment to building high-quality PCEs in the face of a seemingly intractable healthcare dilemma? I advise you to stay educated and tap into your network of professionals no matter how busy you are. Do not let the intensity of project management work cause you to isolate yourself from professional events, new people, and emerging trends. Attend conferences and local trade networking events.

Consider becoming an affiliate member at the CHD, which offers its members useful tools, evidence-based research, resources, and a list of educational and networking events to help you manage your projects, deal with your organization, and mentor your team.

It is worth coming back to Germaine for what she thinks it will take to right the healthcare ship. "There is no silver bullet for healing the healthcare crisis in this country. The people coming to the table to discuss how this will transpire will need to be diverse. They will be traditional healers from varied backgrounds, conventional practitioners, and creative, think-outside-the-box visionaries—people who are not wedded to for-profit models. As we see unlikely social movements such as #MeToo, #NeverAgain, and #BLM ... so will a similar 'revolution' transpire with healthcare. The groundwork has been laid. The power brokers have been put on notice. Whether it is the opioid crisis, the fiscal collapse of Medicare, Medicaid (or both) or the final reckoning that 28 million citizens are uninsured and 31 million are underinsured, is still to be known. But, it is a foregone conclusion that this issue will find its time and soon."[12]

Germaine's ideas, attitude, and trust issues reflect those of many Americans who have reached a tipping point regarding healthcare. Our job is to listen to the stories, understand the attitudes, look at the evidence, and view ideas with openness. We must be the catalyst for change as we strive to build ideal environments that support the medical professional/patient connection, never allowing a patient to walk into an examination room, blood lab, or MRI suite and perceive the experience as a corporate, mechanical, or regimented one. Respect the evergreen principles of *Healthy Patient* by creating an environment that benefits everyone, from the patient who is cared for and valued to the healthcare system that can stay profitable while maintaining its high standards of care and forward growth momentum.

Healthy Patient 2.0

Even with the challenges we face in the U.S. healthcare industry, significant advances have been made in data sharing, digital technology, and patient engagement regarding medical treatment, wellness, and preventive health practices. So how will *Healthy Patient* manifest itself in the future? I predict that healthcare systems will one day resemble university campuses where patients are taught how to best care for their bodies, minds, and spirits. Everyday people will become "students of health," accessing knowledge hubs, programs, services, and experts to understand and address their health concerns and needs. In the process, they will discover their connection to each other, to other living things, and to the planet itself. They will embrace the value of reinforcing these connections and the reality that they are ultimately responsible for their own actions or inactions when it comes to their health and well-being.

What could be better than a healthcare destination that offers a comprehensive approach to self-care through assessment, engagement in a care program, transformation of the recovery experience, and the pursuit of a higher degree of good health? Such a setting makes sense from a *Healthy Patient* standpoint and represents a logical progression in thinking. We are already seeing the development of self-care technologies, such as wearable gadgets that promote accountability for physical activity and caloric intake, and weight-loss monitors that motivate users to comply with performance level expectations. The concept of self-care should be reflected in physical healthcare settings, where a talented, tuned-in team can enhance the patient experience. A well-designed PCE includes technology—whether digital or based on the five senses—that helps teams and patients connect with each other and build trusting relationships. The specific areas of focus that follow are worth attention.

THE CULTURE OF INNOVATION

In a promising development to benefit *Healthy Patient,* healthcare systems and companies that serve the healthcare industry are navigating the competitive terrain by establishing business "incubation" and "accelerator" divisions and programs that fund promising start-ups and supply them with expert mentors who help them move their ideas from vision to reality. And there is no better time for entrepreneurs to be entering the healthcare marketplace with their technological solutions for better engaging patients and for improving the areas of virtual care, medical device design, and consumer digital health services.

Business incubator and accelerator companies understand that the key to survival in the marketplace is to always stay ahead of the curve by leveraging tools, technologies, and workflow methods. Johnson & Johnson Innovation JLABS is leading in this area with eight incubation divisions in North America. To hear it from them, since 2012, JLABs has been providing "the optimal environment for emerging companies to catalyze growth and optimize their research and development by opening them to vital industry connections, delivering entrepreneurial programs and providing a capital-efficient, flexible platform where they can transform the scientific discoveries of today into the breakthrough healthcare solutions of tomorrow."[13]

In another example of nurturing innovation in healthcare, Cedars-Sinai Health System has made entrepreneur mentoring a part of its community benefit mission. To strengthen its relationship with the start-up community, it launched the Cedars-Sinai Accelerator in 2015 in partnership with Techstars, an organization that offers mentorship-driven accelerator programs. Early stage companies that join Techstars' three-month program are provided with funding, mentorship from executives and clinicians, access to Cedars-Sinai, and the opportunity to network with investors and other entrepreneurs.

Finally, innovation can come amid the new era of consumerism from companies that partner with healthcare systems to offer benefits that cater to their employees' needs. Western Digital —a large employer in the St. Joseph Health market in Irvine, California—approached the system in 2017 when it needed a digital health tool for its millennial workforce. Together with St. Joseph's technology partner, Hart, the hospital created an app that Western Digital employees could use to access their own medical records, lab results, discharge information, and other health information.

Clearly there is much to be excited about regarding healthcare innovations. Everyone has a stake in the game and is watching, including Wall Street, which loves to back innovation.

THE HUMAN TOUCH

When addressing healthcare challenges regarding access, costs, delivery modes, and quality outcomes, remember that healthcare cannot be *all* business because it is not at all like other businesses. Moreover, there are pockets of unique needs and considerations that have not yet been lifted by the tide of patient-centered philosophies and approaches.

For example, healthcare approaches in the areas of behavioral health and mental illness have not changed much since the 1980s. Many behavioral health units still have locked areas with isolation rooms and no meaningful access to the outdoors. Gerry Giordano, a former florist, became a behavioral health nurse in 2003. He is also a person with notable talents as a yoga instructor, a craftsman who builds guitars, and a talented weekend musician, and he applies his rich life experience to his work with patients because he believes that professionals in his field should be authentic.

Most patients who receive behavioral health services are acutely aware of and sensitive to their environment, including their caregiver's attitude, which can affect the fostering of cooperation and facilitation of progress. As Gerry noted, "Luckily, I think my background collectively as a musician and yoga teacher allows me to be in the moment. ... I'm in the moment all the time, and you have to be aware and you have to treat the patient with a little bit of dignity and compassion all the time because they see right through and recognize when you are real."[14]

I bring up behavioral health because it is a specialty area requiring an understanding of healing and a balance of process, which takes us back to the need to define who patients are and what they need in their environments to keep them safe and maintain their well-being. From our perspective as builders of PCEs, our actions should ensure that the environment we create is a springboard for delivering the right care at the right time. We can do this by, first and foremost, adhering to a *Healthy Patient* mindset, including understanding the impact that design choices will have on the patient population. The designed space for a behavioral health PCE should support staff, encourage patient and family participation, and facilitate communication, collaboration, and trust. The use of light and sound should be thoughtfully planned out, given some patient sensitivities. The space should include areas where people can gather for discussions or to share meals. Privacy is a top concern, as is access to outdoor space for physical activity. Anything that furthers the creation of an environment that encourages wellness for the long term will help patients transition more successfully to living a healthy life once home.

BACK TO NATURE

In his work, *The Anatomy of Human Destructiveness,* German-born American psychoanalyst Erich Fromm referred to the term biophilia ("the passionate love of life and of all that is alive") and more specifically to the existence of a "biophilic force" in the human psyche that connects us with other species and creates in us a desire to be close to nature. Fromm stated that this force creates a flow that keeps us healthy, but that if we disconnect from nature we become ill.

Considering the effect that mountains, forests, oceans, deserts, and other natural settings can have on our mental well-being, why do many hospitals, particularly those that offer behavioral health services, lack roof gardens, walking paths, or patios? Ignoring the biophilia "love of nature" trend, which is gaining a stronger foothold in the healthcare industry, is imprudent. Imagine a company whose consumer base needs access to the outdoors to maintain wellness. If the company does not supply this access, it will go under.

Fortunately, designers are harnessing the power of the natural world to instill a sense of calm, safety, and well-being in end users of environments, especially in behavioral health settings. A good example of creating a PCE that emphasizes safety while still providing an uplifting environment for patients, families, and staff is the Child and Adolescent Psychiatric Stabilization Unit at Surrey Memorial Hospital in British Columbia, Canada. The space for this specialized short-stay unit, which serves children and teenagers with urgent mental health issues, had originally been the site of the emergency department with only one exterior window. The architecture firm worked collaboratively with the clinicians and used a Lean-based planning process to reconfigure the space into a spacious multipurpose lounge and area for dining and supporting patient activities, with care paid to acoustics, lighting, and furniture.

Finally, when it comes to more broadly supporting the health and wellness of people in built environments, an interesting partnership between two standards organizations is worth a special mention here. The International Living Future Institute and the International WELL Building Institute work together "to promote the design, construction, and operations of health and restorative buildings" by looking for opportunities to align their respective ratings systems, which are the Living Building Challenge and the WELL Building Standard.[15]

DOCTORS ON DEMAND

To address the needs of people who cannot access specialty care because they are limited geographically or socioeconomically, or who might prefer more discreet health services, many healthcare systems are seeing success with telemedicine, whereby mobile and wireless platforms provide a patient with control regarding when and where services are accessed.

For example, some Texas communities struggle to provide care for their underserved and at-risk population. UTMB Health (University of Texas Medical Branch) offers telemedicine and telehealth technologies and addresses issues of access to care. Real-time monitoring and physician-patient interactions eliminate barriers to care for people who live in remote areas and address the lack of specialty or subspecialty providers.

UTMB Health's successful telepsychiatry pediatric care program makes it possible to care for patients who would not normally be able to see a psychiatrist. "In a recent survey of 530 parents whose children received pediatric telepsychiatry care from UTMB Health, an overwhelming 88.5 percent reported that telemedicine made it easier for them to receive treatment by a specialist and more than 60 percent reported better changes in overall functioning for their children after receiving telepsychiatric services."[16]

Looking to the future, there will doubtless be exciting developments regarding access to high-quality medical care. And payers are reimbursing these services as they see the volume of virtual video consultations between patients and primary care physicians increasing (and estimated to double by 2020, according to a Forbes.com article[17]). On-demand service providers include Pager, whose app allows patients to access urgent care services, including finding a local doctor and scheduling in-home visits or virtual telemedicine appointments. Physicians use the service to share patient data across networks, monitor their patients, and manage appointments.

How does this relate to the future of *Health Well Done*? As offerings of digital health services broaden, the comprehensive and customized approaches that healthcare systems develop will inform how their delivery environments are designed and built. There are many important details to get just right, including lighting, sound, privacy, nonglare paint colors, video quality, and high-speed connectivity, to support the virtual visit and arrive at a correct diagnosis and proper treatment plan.

INTEGRATIVE MEDICINE

By now, Americans understand that a healthcare system centered around the treatment of injury and disease is not going to make or keep them healthy. Patients are taking alternate routes, to find practices that prevent illness, and they are willing to pay out of pocket to do so. The National Center for Complementary and Integrative Health reported that between 2002 and 2012, the use rates for chiropractic, acupuncture, and massage therapies increased among people who were not covered by insurance for such care.[18]

Stamford Hospital's Center for Integrative Medicine & Wellness in Connecticut, which my team and I built, treats illnesses that include anxiety, depression, autoimmune disease, irritable bowel syndrome, osteoarthritis, neuropathy, fibromyalgia, pelvic pain, and rheumatoid arthritis. It also provides management for head, neck, and low back pain, stress, and urinary incontinence. Approaches used include acupuncture, trigger point injections, nutritional and supplement counseling, and mind-body therapies.

The exams rooms that we designed are open, calming spaces decorated with a coastal theme. Each has an exam table that doubles as a flat table for acupuncture and massage, and a rolling cart that holds needles and massage oils. We installed dimmable lights and an iPhone speaker system to promote relaxation. The interior waiting room is also used as an education/therapy room where patients can discuss their chronic illness. The yoga room, which overlooks an herb garden, doubles as a test kitchen for cooking classes. In addition, the center is located next to a pharmacy that works with the chief physician to compound remedies made from the garden's herbs. Our team enjoyed building the spa/medical space. We created an environment that offers a combined conventional medicine and alternative therapies approach that make patients feel well cared for.

Despite the potential benefits of complementary and alternative approaches to care, however, few U.S. healthcare systems have fully integrated them into their healthcare delivery models, instead retrofitting them into their Western healthcare delivery models or bypassing them entirely. This can result in a potential loss of patients and revenue for a hospital system that sticks only to conventional treatments. In contrast, *Healthy Patient* reflects added value, better outcomes, better patient engagement, and less cost, achieved by taking a customized integrative medicine approach. Unfortunately, a truly comprehensive and integrative book on functional medicine has yet to be written.

ARTIFICIAL INTELLIGENCE

In his video *ED Visions of 2080,* John Huddy, the founder of Huddy Healthcare Solutions who has worked with more than 300 healthcare organizations on healthcare analytics and facility planning and design, ambitiously re-imagines an emergency care center of the future, where human interaction leads the delivery of care and technology supports it. His highly detailed simulation offers a fascinating walkthrough of sci-fi-like features: an "initiation" portal for retinal scans; "vert pods" (that monitor patients sitting in "omni-directional recliners"); robot assistants; telemedicine kiosks and personal data ports; opaque holographic walls for patient privacy; personalized signage accessed through a patient's retinal code; self-guided transport vehicles; and rejuvenating therapy pods, among others.[19]

Although Huddy's conceptualization is a product of unlimited imagination, we are nevertheless at an exciting crossroads regarding the application of artificial intelligence (AI) in the area of healthcare. For example, in the Guangong Second Provincial General Hospital in China, AI technologies have been incorporated into a number of operations, including pre-diagnostics, imaging, patient records, and supply transportation. Patients use their smartphones to access an "AI doctor," list their symptoms and disease history, and then receive a preliminary diagnosis. According to a hospital spokesperson, the robot is capable of diagnosing more than 200 diseases at an accuracy rate of more than 90 percent, which is at the same proficiency level required of a senior surgeon."[20]

PROJECT MANAGER AS HERO

My hope as a project manager who has seen it all is that you keep an eye out for trends that benefit your PCE project. Why lose patients to the competition when you can instead be the project manager who attracts them to your healthcare setting by respecting their beliefs and fulfilling their needs and wants? The good news for you is that change might well be seeded in the types of projects that C-suite decision makers will assign to you for planning and implementation. At these critical junctures, you have the opportunity to shape and guide the final outcome— perhaps ways unimagined by administrators and purse holders. As you take on these projects, it will benefit you to have kept up with new research, evolving technologies and treatments, and new modes of healthcare delivery, which will be critical for staying true to the spirit of *Healthy Patient*.

Healthy Team 2.0

Thomas Jung, a good friend with 30 years of healthcare regulatory experience, once wrote to me that, "Even the best ingredients don't ensure a fine meal if guidance isn't provided to facilitate when, where, and how each item is utilized. Similarly, a wealth of talented experts can't ensure a successful healthcare project without a coordinating process to optimize their efforts."[21] I have consistently emphasized this philosophy throughout *Health Well Done*. A *Healthy Team* cannot work in a silo. A successful, sustainable PCE can only come from having the big-picture viewpoint that everything is connected.

Future healthcare delivery will continue to be a team-based endeavor involving physicians, nurses, technicians, department heads, administrative staff, volunteers, and patients and their families. Remember to continue practicing inclusivity with these stakeholders as you refine your project management approach to account for innovations and trends that support team collaboration. And when taking on future PCE projects, make sure that every consideration and detail of a project reflects healthcare trends in human resources, including the impact of a multigenerational workforce and fierce industry competition for qualified job candidates. Design decisions made for a working environment should support experienced older workers while simultaneously and aggressively attracting younger talent.

Equally important for managing project teams is staying on top of, and learning from, "trend disrupters," the movers and shakers of business—Warren Buffett, Jamie Dimon, and Jeff Bezos, to name a few—who are creating ripple effects throughout the healthcare industry as they try to crack the "quality healthcare nut" through simple streamlined models. These visionaries all believe that collaboration is the key to all success. In an Inc.com article, Jeff Bezos stated, "There's no lone genius who figures it all out and sends down the magic formula. You study, you debate, you brainstorm, and the answers start to emerge."[22]

Motivating your team will also never go out of style. Fox News Business writer Michael Lee Stallard explained Warren Buffett's talent for motivating people and how he does it by communicating pride and confidence in his people, modeling civility and respect for others, and being approachable and open.[23] Meanwhile, Jamie Dimon, who believes that learning should be a lifetime commitment, "spends 50 percent of his time either reading, talking to people or traveling and this keeps him on top of things."[24]

Finally, all three influential business leaders believe that the way you deal with failure will determine whether you succeed. In his 2010 commencement speech at Syracuse University, Dimon remarked, "Some of the greatest people of all times ... I'm thinking of Nelson Mandela, Indira Gandhi and many others ... have faced enormous setbacks and have persevered, often against seemingly impossible odds" and that, "It takes humility and humanity to be accountable."[25]

These visionaries, with their wisdom and outlook on conducting business, might well fundamentally transform the delivery of healthcare as we know it, so stay tuned and keep an eye on how they manage their teams.

EVOLVING TECHNOLOGIES

As project managers of PCEs, we constantly seek technologies that can improve the healthcare experience for patients and providers. But we might sometimes forget the ways in which they can affect leaders and their teams. As our industry becomes more sophisticated in using cutting-edge project management platforms and data repositories, these tools will exert a greater influence on how we manage our projects, making it essential to have access to the right information at the right time. This is the key to managing project information, such as budgets and schedules, and overall expectations and perspectives.

There are great team communication technology trends under way. In addition to Zoom teleconferencing, which I have already covered in this book, I recommend Slack, a fast, efficient, cloud-based collaboration tool that eliminates the need for e-mail and group chats by serving as a centralized communication hub. Through a URL or invitation, project team members can join Slack to message each other and share documents and images. Slack also accommodates the integration of other services, such as Google Drive and Dropbox. Given the challenges of some project management databases, including with licenses, permission levels, and non-user-friendly interfaces, I believe that more "collaboration friendly" products will hit the market to foster better connectivity, team management, and team relationships.

Another great development resource that I highly recommend for project managers who want to make their meetings actionable is Voicera, an AI-based "meeting assistant" app that works on voice recognition technology to "takes notes" on meeting highlights, including action items. Voicera will then e-mail you the meeting notes that you can edit and share with your team.

Although the rapid evolution of business technologies such as Voicera and Slack can be exciting, if you are a Baby Boomer like me, you might find that the lightning speed of their development can occasionally frustrate your attempts to manage a team, your client's expectations, and a project's requisites and realities. When I started working at Columbia University Irving Medical Center, I was given a PC laptop, an iPad, and an iPhone. These multiple, sometimes incompatible, platforms presented me with challenges, but they also created opportunities to forge connections with my team.

For example, I once saw a savvy Gen-Xer coworker, Dejan, use a Surface Pro to project his presentation during a team meeting. It was exactly what I wanted to do, and so after the meeting I asked him how I could connect my iPad to the cloud and access information from my desktop. Although I was successful, it took several steps and overcoming obstacles, including dealing with firewalls, which was frustrating. Nevertheless, the unforeseen benefit of figuring out how to streamline the way I managed my project information was that I learned something about a team member's knowledge, which could be useful in delivering on my project.

Counted among evolving technologies should be social media. Although we do not tend to think of social media as being relevant for team-based communication, platforms such as Facebook,

Twitter, and Instagram will continue to evolve in how they are used, including to create buzz about a project, solicit feedback, and share project ideas. In addition, business networking platforms such as LinkedIn are always growing their offerings. Keep track of new developments in this area.

Finally, one particularly notable technological trend in the healthcare industry, which should figure into any project plan of the future, is the commonplace use of mobile devices and apps by healthcare professionals at the point of care. Smartphones and tablets with computing power that can put antiquated hospital data systems to shame are transforming the way providers are doing their jobs, thanks to a wealth of available programs and apps. Time and information management apps, clinical practice apps, drug reference guides, medical calculators, support aids for decision making, surgical simulations, hearing and visions tests, and so on, are available through the App Store, Google Play, or directly from custom developers.

LONG-DISTANCE RELATIONSHIPS

Many industries are relying on telecommuting to attract quality talent, reduce a company's environmental footprint, and access a global workforce. As healthcare systems branch out to new countries, project teams will very likely reflect international specialties. Your ability to run a teleconference and deal with different languages and new job titles will greatly matter in keeping everyone on track and communicating. Be proactive in finding ways to address these challenges.

When managing an international team, have someone available to translate procedures and customs. A friend of mine was involved in building same-day surgery centers located in India. A key factor that contributed to her success was her understanding of the social mores centered around surgery in that country. For example, it is customary for large groups of friends and family members to visit a person in the hospital throughout their time in recovery. For the novel concept of same-day surgery to be accepted, and in turn allow the centers to succeed, my friend had to lay down some necessary groundwork, including targeting younger, more progressive-thinking patients who were accepting of the concept of same-day surgery.

Never wait until you are on an actual teleconference video meeting to realize that you are out of your element. Plan ahead, anticipate challenges, and communicate with your team members early and often.

Healthy Project 2.0

As healthcare systems shift from being fixers to preventers, new areas of growth might well drive the types of projects that you take on. According to Kathryn Berger of the Harvard T. H. Chan School of Public Health, "Organizations are taking on projects to incorporate new elements into their workflows, improve processes at every stage of the continuum of care, and enhance their facilities while improving outcomes and decreasing costs. According to the Massachusetts Hospital Association, the benefit of using project management in healthcare is 'to be one step ahead of any potential risk' as they complete this vast array of projects.'"[26]

In light of Berger's statement, it is reassuring to know that the strength and versatility of *Healthy Project* is that it will always provide you with a reliable foundation of evergreen methodologies for addressing any trend, innovation, or challenge that comes your way. Nevertheless, what follows are trends and growing needs requiring greater consideration when striving to achieve a *Healthy Project.*

THE AGING POPULATION

For more than a century, research and social policy have centered on increasing the human life span, with the average U.S. life span increasing from less than 50 years in 1900 to nearly 80 years today.[27] According to the U.S. Census Bureau, by 2030 baby boomers will be older than 65, which will increase the older population so that one in every five Americans is projected to be of retirement age.[28] However, the priority for maximizing years lived is giving way to a greater, concurrent goal. As Baby Boomers retire to enjoy generally longer life expectancies, they are keen on making their later years active, fulfilling, and productive. For them, the goal is not only about increased life span (the length of time one is alive, or kept alive), but also about health span (how long one is truly healthy and thriving). The emphasis being placed on living an optimally healthy life is triggering innovative thinking in the healthcare industry, particularly regarding preventive care and quality-of-life services for elder populations.

One interesting and closely watched effort involves strengthening the fabric of multigenerational societies by establishing symbiotic partnerships between demographic groups, which has demonstrated benefits for young and old alike. For example, an opinion piece in *The Japan Times* discussed a 2013 study that found that bringing together children from a nursery school and residents from a home for the elderly had many unexpected benefits.

Compared to a control group, seniors exhibited greater social interactions, a delay in mental decline, and improvements to their physical health, including a reduction in disease risk and death. The respect and empathy that the young children developed by interacting with seniors appeared to benefit them socially and personally as well.[29]

Another successful example of bridging the generational divide is the LiveWell intergenerational community concept, which is a model of living based on a "co-home" setting for both young people who are aging out of foster care and an older adult population. The LiveWell intergenerational community is designed to promote meaningful relationships between two vulnerable populations, provide mentorship, and create job opportunities that teach youth the life skills necessary for successful outcomes. At-risk youth undergo career development by being part of a "teaching and research" community that provides older adults with quality care and services. The youth are prepared for the workforce while older adults have the opportunity to live purposeful, capable lives.

Aging in place—allowing the elderly to live in their preferred residence for as long as they are able, and with the support services they need, as they age—is proving to be a viable option for allowing individuals to control the quality of their lives and remain independent. Because of associated improvements in health span, senior living project development is on the rise to meet the growing demands for aging in place. Recognizing the importance of optimizing quality outcomes for both the residents and staff of elder-care communities, the organization With Seniors in Mind, composed of volunteers from various backgrounds, developed the "Senior Living Sustainability Guide," a process guide for designing and building sustainable senior living environments that promote a high quality of life for residents as well as staff satisfaction.

These aforementioned projects are particularly suited for a *Health Well Done* management approach. By putting individuals and their needs front and center from project initiation through to close out, a project manager and team will succeed in creating optimal care environments.

DESIGN INDUSTRY INNOVATIONS

Rosalyn Cama, president and principal interior designer at Cama, Inc., which specializes in evidence-based design, believes that as the trend toward preventive health and wellness grows for providers in an era of risk-averse affordable care, the need to discover new ways to build health-oriented spaces will be more urgent. Commercial entities are turning to novel approaches to answer the call for employee wellness.

In March 2018, I participated in Interior Design Media's Health and Wellness Roundtable, which explored how the design industry is integrating wellness into modern design practices and the challenges of doing so. View Dynamic Glass, a manufacturer of "smart glass" and a sponsor of the roundtable, provided case-study research to back up the value of the WELL Building Standard. Their study of 300 people concluded that natural light improves worker health and productivity, with workers reporting a reduction in eyestrain (51 percent), drowsiness (56 percent), and headaches (63 percent).[30] This improvement equates to an additional $100,000 of added annual value for every 100 employees (assuming an average salary of $50,000).[31]

Why should we focus so much of our energy on building PCE environments that reduce eyestrain, prevent headaches, and decrease drowsiness in the healthcare staff? (Remember the *Healthy Project* component of *Health Well Done* begins with the "why" behind the project.) Because not only is it the right thing to do for the well-being of staff, but because happier, more productive workers are more likely to take better care of patients. I recommend that you introduce and explain this vision at the very beginning of a project and include the relevant line items in your budget and schedule to reflect a dedication to employee wellness.

INFECTIOUS DISEASE CONTROL

In the never-ending efforts by healthcare systems to address infectious disease control, something as simple as hand hygiene plays a critical role in keeping everyone safe and less susceptible to infection and contagious disease. Approximately 1.7 million healthcare-associated infections (HAIs) occur in U.S. hospital systems each year, resulting in 99,000 deaths and about $20 billion in healthcare costs.[32] On any given day in the United States, about 1 out of every 25 patients will acquire at least one infection during their stay in a hospital.[33] In addition to the risk posed to patients, healthcare systems are paying the price. In 2017, Medicare evaluated 3,306 hospitals and penalized 751 of them for HAIs.[34]

Clearly, the issue of infectious disease control will figure prominently in the future of *Health Well Done*. Both large and small project management decisions on safety will have a direct impact on controlling the spread of disease, making it vital for project managers to pay careful attention to infection control details. Wesley Hawkins, director of healthcare design for M+A Architects, advises that you start by having a conversation about how to marry company culture with functional, purposeful PCE design elements. Applied to infection control, this could mean ensuring that handwashing sinks are highly visible in in-patient care areas to prompt staff to follow procedure; educating staff on handwashing; and installing antimicrobial surfaces and easy-to-clean materials. Moreover, addressing HVAC concerns—the quality of air flow, filtration, humidity, ventilation velocity, and pressure—and the maintenance of mechanical, electrical, and plumbing (MEP) systems, is vital for inhibiting outbreaks, so make sure to involve your knowledgeable facilities staff.

INTEGRATED PRACTICE UNITS

Looking to the future, we will see a continuation of the trend to organize healthcare around patients' medical conditions. For example, the IPU, or integrated practice unit, is a collaborative patient-centered approach to care that is characterized by a team of providers and support staff who focus on one particular condition or disease. Harvard Business School's Institute for Strategy & Competitiveness (ISC) has identified the transformative principle of "shared value" that IPUs can provide, defined as "creating economic value in a way that also creates value for society by addressing its needs and challenges."[35] Rather than increase the number of services offered, IPUs grow by enhancing and optimizing the focused service they provide to their local communities.

As project managers, we will find ourselves working more often in IPU settings. Six of the 11 key attributes of IPUs listed by the ISC are especially relevant to our PCE project efforts:[36]

1   IPUs are organized around the patient's medical condition.

2   They involve a dedicated, multidisciplinary team that devotes a significant portion of its time to the condition.

3   They take responsibility for the full cycle of care for the condition, encompassing outpatient, in-patient, and rehabilitative care as well as supporting services (for example, nutrition, social work, behavioral health).

4   They incorporate patient education, engagement, and follow-up as integral to care.

5   Providers function as a team, meeting formally and informally on a regular basis to discuss patients, processes, and results.

6   They accept joint accountability for outcomes and costs.

If you are managing an IPU project, your ability to understand the unique requirements of treating different medical conditions, to walk in a patient's shoes, to work with a multidisciplinary team, and to remember the big picture will prove indispensable, particularly when it comes to the expanding areas of rehabilitative care, nutrition (think kitchens and gardens), and education. You will need to consider specialized needs and build them into your PCEs early on in the project. Ask the right questions about scope and vision, your expectations of your team, the organizational culture, and then apply the principles of initiation and planning, the two phases that serve as the springboard to reaching your project goals.

A Healthy Planet Matters, Too

Poet George Krokos has aptly described our life on earth: "There are worlds within worlds in this world of ours." You might be surprised at what this section covers, but it is an area of discussion that should not be overlooked.

As a project manager, you are doubtless keenly aware that facility builds require a carefully considered vision for what will work both in the short term and in 10, 20, or 30 years from now. To ensure comprehensiveness in your planning and execution of a project, you must continually orchestrate the ideas, beliefs, and knowledge of all stakeholders—from clinicians and patients to architects and facilities managers—while balancing them against the needs of the community and planet as a whole.

We have been drilled on the top three reasons to invest in staff wellness: to promote good health, attract and retain quality talent, and enhance productivity. Each of these priorities relates to the human aspects of business, but we also must consider their inextricable link to the broader environment, beyond even the local communities and towns that PCEs serve. The importance of ensuring a *Healthy Planet* (the honorary fourth pillar of *Health Well Done*) is of vital import because the earth is our life support. It keeps us healthy, heals us, enhances our mood, and reduces our stress. As a project manager, you must work to exceed the parameters of the PCE project at hand with an eye toward its connection to the rest of the world.

You can do this by always thinking of steps that you can take throughout the project cycle to incorporate the natural environment into your PCEs and their operation. Examples include going green with LED lighting, building green ("living") roofs, installing high-efficiency HVAC equipment, using recycled rubber flooring, FSC-certified wood, and VOC paints, encouraging a bike-friendly culture, and consolidating data centers for energy efficiency.

These ideas are part of smart-building wellness programs gaining in popularity as cutting-edge technology meets the world of building management. The challenge, however, is that health is difficult to quantify, so it is important to follow standards already established by such organizations as such as WELL, Fitwel (similar to WELL, but with a focus on location, stairwells, and entrances), and RESET (focuses on indoor air quality).

We have to face the fact that owners and facilities departments are tasked with a bigger role in the health and happiness of the people who occupy their buildings, and the best time to ensure that wellness goals and ideas are represented in the final PCE is by incorporating them into a project plan during the initiation and planning phases.

As you move through each phase of your project's life cycle, be ready to take a stand and make a strong business case for ideas that protect the earth. You will win your case if you understand the healthcare system's business goals, which typically align with smart-building wellness programs. Be willing to research, advocate, and implement sustainable practices. After all, what is the use of struggling to keep us all healthy if the planet that sustains us is not healthy? Our interconnectedness—to each other, to other living things, and to Mother Earth—is a fact that we must acknowledge and respect.

The benefits of ecofriendly design are countless, not just for ourselves, but for future generations. Convince decision makers to follow your lead by speaking their language: the bottom line. For example, although an added cost per employee, incorporating the WELL Building Standard into your project can save you more on insurance costs in the long term. Show C-suite executives why this is worthwhile by pointing out the cost of unwellness at work ($2.2 trillion lost annually [12 percent of U.S. GDP] due to costs of chronic disease, work-related injuries and illnesses, work-related stress, and disengagement at work[37]).

We all have a personal accountability toward protecting each other and preserving the planet. By taking these additional steps to consider a *Healthy Planet* in your project management, you will truly arrive at a project well done.

Conclusion

Health Well Done was written for project managers who are committed to leading PCE projects that will make a difference in patients' lives. A big part of achieving success is bringing people together in an atmosphere of collaborative, creative thinking, and inspiring them to commit to a shared mission. Another is recognizing that any one of us can find ourselves seeking care in a PCE at any point in our lives. By walking in the shoes of others, we will be sure to perform our project tasks responsibly and with integrity.

Never forget that your work as a project manager and team leader will have results that reverberate far and wide and for a very long time. Everything that you decide and set into motion will come full circle to connect you with your team members, your team members to the end users, the end users to the resulting PCE, the PCE to its community, the community to the greater society, and society to the planet itself. This is *Health Well Done* in its ideal form, and I hope that the journey we have taken together has provided you with insights and practical advice that will help you join others who are dedicated to being the best possible project managers and to making a difference.

ACKNOWLEDGMENTS

First and foremost, I would like to acknowledge my editor, Mary Kalamaras, for her tireless effort and her passion for getting this topic right, as she has made a huge impact on the quality of the work in this book. I knew after my first conversation with Mary that I wanted to work with her because she understood my vision. The topic of healthcare can at times be dry and boring, but she pushed ahead while preserving the heart of the content.

Second, I would like to thank my husband, Ken, for supporting me throughout the four long years of writing this book, for acting as my sounding board, confidant, and mentor, and for always having my back as I worked to realize this professional and creative vision.

I need to give a shout out to my mom, whom I call "Mother Theresa," who taught me to be dedicated to one's work and family no matter how big or small the challenges faced. Never give up on each other.

To my team who helped me stay focused and get the work done: Sarah Anozier, Christina Chase, Beth Granger, Tanya Preston, Paige Wilhide, and Dharma Kelleher. I could never have launched this book without your help and support, so thank you.

Thanks also go to Lisa Soraghan (book design), Melanie Zimmerman (proofreading), and Jean Jesensky (indexing) for their excellent professional work on this book.

To my friends and colleagues at NSANYC: Thank you for being open to sharing your wisdom and experience with regard to running a speaking business and publishing a book. It is great to see that people are willing to share their knowledge and time to help others become better at their craft.

To my Mastermind group: You ladies have talked me off the ledge many times and lifted me up to successfully face many business challenges, including publishing this book. I am so grateful that you are in my life.

To my friends and colleagues at The Center for Health Design: Thank you for supporting me and making me feel a part of an organization that understands the healthcare industry's challenges, and for showing me that if we work together to remain dedicated to patient care now and in the future, we can only expect healthy outcomes for all of us.

To Stamford Hospital, a high-quality healthcare system: You taught me a whole lot about patient care. I will always be indebted to the doctors and nurses for the VIP care that I received during my ovarian cancer treatment, as well as to my colleagues for their kindness, compassion, and support before, during, and after my treatments.

To my new colleagues at Columbia University Irving Medical Center, and in particular to Patrick Burke and Anthony Donatich: Thank you for supporting me and helping me gain new insights.

To my family who listened, watched, and nodded every time I told them that the book was "coming out very soon": I never clearly understood what it took to write and publish a book, and to this day I am still amazed that I have created this wonderful product. I could have never accomplished this without the support and hard work of all of the wonderful people in my life. I am so very lucky to be surrounded by so many talented and compassionate colleagues, friends, and family.

Last of all, a thank-you goes to my dog and hiking partner, Cali, always by my side as I hiked the Vermont Green Mountain National Forest (my "think tank"), where many of my ideas and visions became reality.

NOTES

INTRODUCTION: THE VALUE OF A HEALTHCARE PROJECT WELL DONE

1   **conditions related to stress:** Benson-Henry Institute, "Integration of Mind Body Medicine into Current Health Care Models," retrieved June 14, 2017, https://www.bensonhenryinstitute.org/mission-history/.

2   **reduced stress in patients and staff:** Roger Ulrich, Craig Zimring, et al. "The Role of the Physical Environment in the Hospital of the 21st Century: A Once-in-a-Lifetime Opportunity," The Center for Health Design, September 2004, retrieved July 31, 2017, https://www.healthdesign.org/system/files/Ulrich_Role%20of%20Physical_2004.pdf.

3   **you will fail a lot:** Taylor Soper, "Amazon's Secrets of Invention: Jeff Bezos Explains How to Build an Innovative Team," Geekwire, May 17, 2016, retrieved August 31, 2017, https://www.geekwire.com/2016/amazons-secrets-invention-jeff-bezos-explains-build-innovative-team/.

4   **always co-created with patients:** Madge Kaplan, "Co-Production: A New Lens on Patient-Centered Care," Institute for Healthcare Improvement, April 1, 2016, retrieved May 14, 2017, http://www.ihi.org/communities/blogs/co-production-a-new-lens-on-patient-centered-care.

CHAPTER 1: HEALTHY PATIENT

1   **performing at their best:** Bruce Japsen, "U.S. Workforce Illness Costs $576B Annually from Sick Days to Workers Compensation," Forbes, September 12, 2012, retrieved August 31, 2017, www.forbes.com/sites/brucejapsen/2012/09/12/u-s-workforce-illness-costs-576b-annually-from-sick-days-to-workers-compensation/#32de29565db0.

2   **the benefit of U.S. business:** Ibid.

3   **suffer fewer post-surgical complications:** Janice Kiecolt-Glaser, Gayle Giboney Page, et al. "Psychological Influences on Surgical Recovery: Perspectives from Psychoneuroimmunology," American Psychologist, 1998, Nov;53(11):1209-18. PMID: 9830373.

4   **improve clinical outcomes:** Ibid.

5   **The categories are:** Lida Lewis, "WELL Building Standard: A Brief Introduction," LinkedIn, September 19, 2015, retrieved August 31, 2017, https://www.slideshare.net/Lida_Lewis/well-building-standard-introduction.6.

6   **then closing this gap:** Leonard L. Berry, Joseph O. Jacobson, et al. "Managing the Clues in Cancer Care," Journal of Oncology Practice, 2016, May;12(5):407-10. PMID: 27006353.

7   **Planetree patient-centered care are:** Susan B. Frampton, Laura Gilpin, et al. (editors), "Putting Patients First: Designing and Practicing Patient-Centered Care," Health Expectations, 2003, Dec;7(4):352-353. Doi: 10.1111/j.1369-7625.2004.00302.x.

8   **heart rate and blood pressure:** Deborah Cracknell, Matthew P. White, et al. "Marine Biota and Psychological Well-Being: A Preliminary Examination of Dose-Response Effects in an Aquarium Setting," Environment and Behavior, 2016, Dec;(10):1242-1269.

CHAPTER 2: HEALTHY TEAM

1   **is its membership:** Harvard Business Review staff, "Five Critical Roles in Project Management," Harvard Business Review, November 3, 2016, retrieved August 27, 2016, https://hbr.org/2016/11/five-critical-roles-in-project-management/.

2   **in a way that lets others relax:** David C. Baker, "Top 10 Characteristics of GREAT Project Managers," 99U, October 27, 2010, retrieved July 12, 2017, http://99u.com/articles/6946/top-10-characteristics-of-great-project-managers.

3   **and finish the project:** Jim Collins, "Level 5 Leadership: The Triumph of Humility and Fierce Resolve," Harvard Business Review, July-August 2005, retrieved January 31, 2018, https://hbr.org/2005/07/level-5-leadership-the-triumph-of-humility-and-fierce-resolve.

4   **than Patton or Caesar:** Jim Collins, From *Good to Great: Why Some Companies Make the Leap ... and Others Don't*, New York: HarperCollins, 2001, p. 13.

5   **A great project manager:** Google re:Work, "Learn about Google's Management Research," retrieved July 12, 2017, https://rework.withgoogle.com/guides/managers-identify-what-makes-a-great-manager/steps/learn-about-googles-manager-research/.

6   **to develop a creative solution:** Becca Nell, personal interview conducted by the author, June 21, 2017.

7   **an effective and accurate observer:** Andrew Cox, "Observation: A Critical Leadership Skill," Ezine Articles, September 20, 2007, retrieved July 17, 2017, http://ezinearticles.com/?Observation---A-Critical-Leadership-Skill&id=743048.

8   **how one presents themselves on the Internet:** Sylvie Di Giusto, "What Do the First 7 Seconds Say About You," Wholesaler Masterminds Radio Show, audio, retrieved July 17, 2017, https://wholesalermasterminds.com/2017/02/the-abcds-of-a-professional-imprint-with-sylvie-di-giusto/.

9   **they figure out where to drive it:** Jim Collins, *From Good to Great*, p. 12.

10 **delays in the execution stage:** Kathryn Berger, "A Primer on Project Management for Health Care," Inside Health, Harvard T. H. Chan School of Public Health, retrieved July 15, 2017, https://www.hsph.harvard.edu/ecpe/a-primer-on-project-management-for-health-care/.

11 **among other benefits:** Avish Parashar, "Business Improv: Turning the Ridiculous into Relevance," Ding Happens! January 31, 2017, retrieved November 1, 2017, http://dinghappens.com/01/business-improv-turning-the-ridiculous-into-relevance/.

12 referred to as the "helper's high": Thupten Jinpa, *A Fearless Heart: How the Courage to Be Compassionate Can Transform Our Lives*, New York: Penguin Group USA, 2015, Kindle edition.

CHAPTER 3: HEALTHY PROJECT

1 good patient care sense: Larry Scanlon, *Hospital Mergers: Why They Work, Why They Don't*, Chicago: AHA Press, 2010, p. 97.

2 the process starts all over again: Debra Levin, "Healthcare Form Meets Healthcare Function," Healthcare Design, July 10, 2015, retrieved May 25, 2017, http://www.healthcaredesignmagazine.com/trends/perspectives/healthcare-form-meets-healthcare-function/.

3 to achieve a potential gain: Phil M. Jones, *Exactly What to Say: The Magic Words for Influence and Impact*, Hoboken, NJ: Box of Tricks Publishing, 2017, p. 25.

4 while you are executing change: Jeffrey Hayzlett and Jim Eber, *Running the Gauntlet: Essential Business Lessons to Lead, Drive Change, and Grow Profits*, New York: McGraw Hill-Education, 2012, p. 10.

CHAPTER 4: THE ART OF STORYTELLING

1 strongly influenced by story: Jonathan Gottschall, "Why Storytelling Is the Ultimate Weapon," Fast Company, May 12, 2012, retrieved May 23, 2017, https://www.fastcompany.com/1680581/why-storytelling-is-the-ultimate-weapon.

2 into the characters' world: Paul J. Zak, "How Stories Change the Brain," Greater Good Magazine, December 17, 2013, retrieved January 11, 2018, https://greatergood.berkeley.edu/article/item/how_stories_change_brain.

3 to need our help: Ibid.

4   **we listen to what you say:** Kelly Swanson, "Why Your Personal
    Story Matters in Business," HuffPost, November 27, 2016, retrieved
    June 12, 2017, http://snip.ly/auw1c#http://www.huffingtonpost.
    com/entry/why-your-personal-story-matters-in-business_
    us_583b2175e4b050dfe6187d17.

CHAPTER 5: WHEN PROJECTS GO AWRY

There are no notes for this chapter.

CHAPTER 6: THE FUTURE OF HEALTH WELL DONE

1   **interventions that link the two:** David Kindig and G. Stoddart,
    "What Is Population Health?" American Journal of Public Health,
    2003, Mar;93(3):371-379, retrieved July 10, 2018, https://ajph.
    aphapublications.org/doi/pdf/10.2105/AJPH.93.3.380.

2   **the most credible form of advertising:** Nielsen,
    "Recommendations from Friends Remain Most Credible Form
    of Advertising Among Consumers: Branded Websites Are the
    Second-Highest-Rated Form," September 28, 2015, retrieved
    May 4, 2018, http://www.nielsen.com/be/en/press-room/2015/
    recommendations-from-friends-remain-most-credible-form-of-
    advertising.html.

3   **and healing environment elements:** The Center for Health
    Design, "Design Solutions to Improve Healthcare Access and
    Outcomes—Adelante Healthcare Mesa," March 2017, retrieved
    July 26, 2018, https://www.healthdesign.org/insights-solutions/
    design-solutions-improve-healthcare-access-and-outcomes-
    adelante-healthcare-mesa.

4   **bringing people together:** The Center for Health Design, "High
    Impact Design Solutions to Improve Healthcare Access and
    Outcomes—Clinica Family Health People's Medical Clinic,"
    March 2017, retrieved July 26, 2018, https://www.healthdesign.
    org/insights-solutions/high-impact-design-solutions-improve-
    healthcare-access-and-outcomes-clinica.

5 **society as a whole:** Milken Institute School of Public Health staff, "What Is Population Health?" Milken Institute School of Public Health, April 27, 2015, retrieved May 4, 2018, https://mha.gwu. edu/what-is-population-health/.

6 **health and wellness:** The Center for Health Design, "Design Solutions to Improve Healthcare Access and Outcomes—Kaiser Permanente Antelope Valley Medical Offices," March 2017, retrieved July 26, 2018, https://www.healthdesign.org/insights-solutions/design-solutions-improve-healthcare-access-and-outcomes-kaiser-permanente.

7 **profit and market share:** Tracy Frisch, "The End of Insurance? Andrew Coates on Fixing Our Broken Healthcare System." The Sun, March 2018, retrieved July 28, 2018, https://www.thesunmagazine.org/issues/507/the-end-of-insurance.

8 **very basic to humanity:** Ibid.

9 **experiencing professional burnout:** Tait D. Shanafelt and John H. Noseworthy, "Executive Leadership and Physician Well-being: Nine Organizational Strategies to Promote Engagement and Reduce Burnout," special article, Mayo Foundation for Medical Education and Research, 2017, Jan;92(1):129-146.

10 **substance abuse, depression, and suicide:** Ibid.

11 **whether physicians remain engaged or burn out:** Ibid.

12 **this issue will find its time and soon:** Germaine Fraser, personal communication with the author, March 3, 2018.

13 **healthcare solutions of tomorrow:** Johnson & Johnson Innovation, "Johnson & Johnson Innovation, JLABS Release Impact Report," October 12, 2017, retrieved July 25, 2018, https://jlabs.jnjinnovation.com/news/johnson-johnson-innovation-jlabs-releases-impact-report.

14 **recognize when you are real:** Gerry Giordano, personal interview conducted by author, March 4, 2018.

15 **the WELL Building Standard:** International WELL Building Institute and International Living Future Institute, "Living Building Challenge & the WELL Building Standard: Approaches for Projects Seeking a Dual Rating," 2017, retrieved July 25, 2018, https://standard.wellcertified.com/sites/default/files/WELL-LBC-Crosswalk-Final-1.pdf.

16 **after receiving telepsychiatric services:** Alexander Vo, George Byron Brooks, et al., "Benefits of Telemedicine in Remote Communities and Use of Mobile and Wireless Platforms in Healthcare," UTMB Health, Retrieved July 25, 2018, https://telehealth.utmb.edu/presentations/Benefits_Of_Telemedicine.pdf.

17 **according to a Forbes article:** Bruce Japsen, "Doctors' Virtual Consults with Patients to Double by 2020," Forbes, August 9, 2015, retrieved July 12, 2018, https://www.forbes.com/sites/brucejapsen/2015/08/09/as-telehealth-booms-doctor-video-consults-to-double-by-2020/#3431bb614f9b.

18 **not covered by insurance for such care:** National Center for Complementary and Integrative Health, "What Complementary and Integrative Approaches Do Americans Use?" Last modified September 24, 2017, retrieved July 10, 2018, https://nccih.nih.gov/research/statistics/NHIS/2012/key-findings.

19 **rejuvenating therapy pods, among others:** Huddy HealthCare Solutions, "ED Vision 2080," video, retrieved July 12, 2018, http://huddyhealthcare.com/ed-vision-2080/.

20 **required of a senior surgeon:** Life of Guangzhou, "Guangzhou Gives Birth to China's Smartest Hospital," updated April 4, 2018, retrieved July 14, 2018, http://www.lifeofguangzhou.com/knowGZ/content.do?contextId=7360&frontParentCatalogId=175.

21 **to optimize their efforts:** Thomas Jung, personal communication with the author, April 13, 2018.

22 **the answers start to emerge:** Samuel Bacharach, "Jeff Bezos' Innovation Formula," Inc., October 17, 2013, retrieved July 29, 2018, https://www.inc.com/samuel-bacharach/jeff-bezos-innovation-formula.html.

23 **being approachable and open:** Michael Lee Stallard, "Warren Buffett's 3 Practices that Attract and Retain Top Talent," Fox News Network, February 27, 2014, retrieved July 29, 2018, https://www.foxbusiness.com/features/warren-buffetts-3-practices-that-attract-and-retain-top-talent.

24 **on top of things:** Leadership Geeks, "Jamie Dimon Leadership Profile," August 10, 2016, retrieved July 13, 2018, http://www.leadershipgeeks.com/jamie-dimon-leadership/.

25 **to be accountable:** News staff, "Remarks by Jamie Dimon at Syracuse University's 156th Commencement and the SUNY College of Environmental Science and Forestry's 113th Commencement," May 16, 2010, retrieved September 14, 2018, https://news.syr.edu/2010/05/commencement-remarks/.

26 **this vast array of projects:** Kathryn Berger, "A Primer on Project Management for Health Care," Harvard T. H. Chan School of Public Health, December 17, 2015, retrieved July 28, 2018, https://www.hsph.harvard.edu/ecpe/a-primer-on-project-management-for-health-care/.

27 **nearly 80 years today:** Eileen M. Crimmins, "Lifespan and Healthspan: Past, Present, and Promise," The Gerontologist, 2015, Dec; 55(6):901-911. Published online November 10, 2015, doi: 10.1093/geront/gnv130.

28 **to be of retirement age:** U.S. Census Bureau, "Older People Projected to Outnumber Children for First Time in U.S. History, press release, September 6, 2018, retrieved September 14, 2018, https://www.census.gov/newsroom/press-releases/2018/cb18-41-population-projections.html.

29 **and personally as well:** Walt Gardner, "Interaction Benefits Toddlers and Elderly Alike," The Japan Times, March 13, 2016, retrieved May 26, 2018, https://www.japantimes.co.jp/opinion/2016/03/13/commentary/japan-commentary/interaction-benefits-toddlers-elderly-alike/#.W5vwfy2ZO_I.

30 **and headaches (63%):** View Dynamic Glass, "Natural Light Is the Best Medicine for the Office," press release, January 31, 2018, retrieved July 27, 2018, https://viewglass.com/assets/pdfs/daylight-research.pdf.

31 **and average salary of $50,000:** Ibid.

32 **$20 billion in healthcare costs:** Centers for Disease Control and Prevention, "CDC at Work: Preventing Healthcare-Associated Infections," retrieved July 2, 2018, https://www.cdc.gov/washington/~cdcatwork/pdf/infections.pdf.

33 **during their stay in a hospital:** Centers for Disease Control and Prevention, "National and State Healthcare Associated Infections Progress Report," 2016, retrieved July 2, 2018, https://www.cdc.gov/HAI/pdfs/progress-report/hai-progress-report.pdf.

34 **of them for (HAIs):** Jeff Lagasse, "Medicare Penalized 751 Facilities for Hospital-Acquired Conditions in 2017," Healthcare Finance News, December 28, 2017, retrieved July 24, 2018, https://www.healthcarefinancenews.com/news/medicare-penalized-751-facilities-hospital-acquired-conditions-2017.

35 **its needs and challenges:** Institute for Strategy and Competitiveness, "Integrating Practice Units: Organizing Care Around Patient Medical Conditions," Harvard Business School, retrieved July 28, 2018, https://www.isc.hbs.edu/health-care/vbhcd/Pages/integrated-practice-units.aspx.

36 **our PCE project efforts:** Ibid.

37 **and disengagement at work:** Global Wellness Institute, "The Future of Wellness at Work," research report, January 2016, retrieved July 28, 2018, https://globalwellnessinstitute.org/press-room/press-releases/global-wellness-institute-releases-report-and-survey-on-the-future-of-wellness-at-work/.

RESOURCES

Managing healthcare projects is not easy. Construction professionals who are constantly facing deadlines often do not have the time to learn or try something new. This is why I created a set of resource documents that augment key information found in *Health Well Done.* It is my hope that these templates, checklists, plans, case studies, and other items will help you better understand and apply the concepts that I have discussed and also serve as adaptable starting points for your own project-specific circumstances. You can download them at http://healthwelldone.com/resources/.

CHAPTER 1: HEALTHY PATIENT

Involving Staff at the Front Lines (page 52): The *Healthy Patient Checklist* is useful for hearing about patient needs from the staff members who run the facility's daily operations. The *HCAHPS Report Card* measures patient satisfaction, making it important for the staff to know the types of questions that patients will be asked and to consider what the responses might be. Gathering this information will ensure that suitable strategies are implemented for delivering optimal patient care. During the project initiation phase, ask the frontline staff to complete the checklist and to read the *HCAHPS Report Card* so that important feedback can be reflected in the final project design.

CHAPTER 2: HEALTHY TEAM

Complying with Rules and Requirements (page 85): The decisions made during the early stages of a project will have a significant impact on the project's outcome. A functional program is a useful way to document project requirements, constraints, and design decisions. It should be developed by an interdisciplinary design team that includes the staff members who will look after the facility once it is built. Use the *Functional Program Keys* resource to guide your program development and explain the benefits of a functional program to your team.

CHAPTER 3: HEALTHY PROJECT

Mock-Up Rooms (page 132): A mock-up room simulates what a proposed space will look like and how it will function. When reviewed with end users, it provides invaluable functional feedback about any issues or potential problems involving equipment, siting, and other concerns that might otherwise be overlooked. Use a drawing of a single room layout and ask end users to talk through each step of their work process in that space. The *Mock-Up Room Questionnaire Example* includes drawings and sample questions to guide your own mock-up process. (Many thanks go to Roseann Pisklak, principal of EYP Health, for allowing me the use of this helpful tool.)

Completing Construction Paperwork (page 135): The *Infection Control Risk Assessment (ICRA)* and *Interim Life Safety Measures (ILSM)* are documents that remain live throughout a project and dictate how infection risks are controlled and what administrative actions are taken to temporarily compensate for the hazards posed by construction activities. Project managers must include

ICRA and ILSM criteria in their bid documents to ensure that contractors account for any costs that these requirements add to the budget. Before construction begins, the contractor should also submit to you an ICRA plan, so that the infection prevention nurse can sign off on the ICRA permit. Your project team also needs to work with the facility and safety officer to determine ILSM requirements for each unique project circumstance. Finally, architects should follow the Facility Guideline Institute's guidelines (https://www.fgiguidelines.org) for the type of building being designed by addressing ICRA and ILSM requirements in their design plans, including demonstrating how they have mitigated infection risks and recording what hazards remain.

Tending to Your Budget (page 136): A well-considered budget is crucial to keeping your project and team on track. Here are two templates to get you started:

Draft Budget: Use this template to monitor your own project budget. Swap in your own line items for a ready-made budget.

Budget Assumptions: It is worthwhile to record any assumptions that you have made during your budget preparation to refer to them later as the project progresses. This document shows you examples of what assumptions to include in your budget.

Creating a Hard-Working Schedule (page 138): The *Schedule Template* is used to track actions—who is doing what and when they are supposed to finish it. It will keep track of construction activities and anything else that can affect the project. Make sure to update your schedule during meetings to be able to adjust your team's activities as needed.

Modes of Communication (page 144): It is worth establishing communication protocols with your team up front, as well as decide on what to do if communication breaks down. In this way, everyone is clear about what, and how, they should communicate with others. When used during the project initiation meetings, the *Communication Plan* and the *Mediation Plan* will help you discuss procedures with your team and get everyone's buy-in.

Installing or Removing Equipment (page 156): When it comes removing or installing complex equipment, a project manager needs to be certain that all technical and procedural requirements are met. For example, a cryogen vent and cooling system for an MRI suite must be installed prior to the MRI machine's installation. Check equipment manuals for installation or removal prerequisites and make sure that the architect has all the information he or she needs to complete design plans. GE Healthcare's *SIGNA Architect, Discovery MR 750W Preinstallation Manual* for magnetic resonance imaging equipment will give you an idea of the types of issues you might need to address.

Creating a Mediation Plan (pages 156 and 211): See "Modes of Communication."

Preparing a Close-Out Checklist (page 161): The project close-out package consists of documents—financials, as-built drawings, manuals, signed-off punch lists, inspection certificates, etc.—handed over to the owner of the space to serve as a formal recognition that the project is complete and to provide the assurance that the work performed meets all applicable standards. A close-out package also reduces your company's risk by confirming that all required documents have been delivered, leaving your client with a good impression of your work as the project manager. Use the *Close-Out Checklist* as a guide for your close-out procedure.

CHAPTER 4: THE ART OF STORY TELLING

Case Studies (page 184): Case studies are a familiar and effective way to help your team members get into the mindset needed for creating patient-centered healthcare environments by encouraging them to consider how a patient felt about the care they received and the challenges they faced during their healthcare experience. The *Case Study Example* will show you how to use the SPA Approach to identify the characters, story points, and applications of a healthcare-related story. I have also included *Case Study 1* and *Case Study 2* for you to use with your team.

Patient Relations Testimonials (page 195): Patient testimonials are a useful resource for gleaning insights into creating an optimal patient-centered environment. Armed with information on what patients like or dislike, the project team can address needs during the design phase. Use the *Testimonial Worksheet* to turn your testimonials into a story (case study) that helps members identify the main points of concern so that thoughtful solutions can be incorporated into both the design and function of a space.

CHAPTER 5: WHEN PROJECTS GO AWRY

Blow-by-Blow Reports (page 222): Every time you speak to a team member, supplier, contractor, or owner about a project, you should record the outcome, especially if an important decision is made, because you might one day find yourself having to provide details of key communications and decisions to others, including the C-suite. The *Blow-by-Blow Description Template* will show you how to stay informed and on top of things.

Handling Project Controls (page 230): A monthly project summary report distills critical project information from various source documents, including meeting minutes, reports, and budgets, into one master document. By gathering together disparate data, you will better manage project controls by having a clear overview of where the project is headed and what issues might need resolving. Schedule time in your calendar for the end of each month to create your summary. The *Project Summary Template* is a basic layout that includes a sample of information items to include and can be customized for your own needs.

RECOMMENDED READING

GENERAL BUSINESS

Arden, Paul. *It's Not How Good You Are, It's How Good You Want to Be.* New York: Phaidon Press, 2003.

Cleary, Thomas. *The Book of Leadership and Strategy: Lessons of the Chinese Masters.* Boston: Shambhala Publications, 1990.

Coffman, Lynn and Michael Valentine. *Slay the Email Monster: 96 Easy Ways to Dramatically Increase Productivity.* Lynn Coffman and Michael Valentine, 2010.

Costa, Rebecca D. *The Watchman's Rattle: A Radical New Theory of Collapse.* New York: Vanguard Press, 2012.

Courville, Roger. *The Virtual Presenter's Playbook: 250 Ideas for Rocking Your Next Webinar, Webcast, or Virtual Class.* Troutville, OR: 1080 Group, 2015.

Goleman, Daniel. *Emotional Intelligence: Why It Can Matter More Than IQ.* New York: Bantam Books, 1995.

Goleman, Daniel, Richard E. Boyatzis and Annie McKee. *Primal Leadership: Realizing the Power of Emotional Intelligence.* Boston: Harvard Business Review Press, 2002.

Harnish, Verne. *Scaling Up: How a Few Companies Make It ... and Why the Rest Don't.* Ashburn, VA: Gazelles, 2014.

Hayzlett, Jeffrey, with Jim Eber. *Running the Gauntlet: Essential Business Lessons to Lead, Drive Change, and Grow Profits.* New York: McGraw-Hill, 2011.

Hogshead, Sally. *How the World Sees You: Discover Your Highest Value Through the Science of Fascination.* New York: HarperBusiness, 2014.

Horsager, David. *The Trust Edge: How Top Leaders Gain Faster Results, Deeper Relationships, and a Stronger Bottom Line.* New York: Free Press, 2012.

Latz, Jane. *Communicate Up the Corporate Ladder: How to Succeed in Business with Clarity and Confidence.* Oceanside, CA: Indie Books International, 2016.

LeBlanc, Mark. *Growing Your Business! What You Want to Know, What You Need to Do.* 2nd ed. Andover, MN: Expert Publishing, 2003.

Lencioni, Patrick M. *The Advantage: Why Organizational Health Trumps Everything Else in Business.* San Francisco: Jossey-Bass, 2012.

Lutze, Heather F. *Marketing Espionage: How to Spy on Yourself, Your Prospects and Your Competitors to Dominate Online.* Parker, CO: Findability Group, 2018.

Nelson, Don. *Challenge the Leader Inside: You Have What It Takes to Be a Genuine Leader.* Tony, WI: Publishers ExpressPress, 2014.

Pink, Daniel H. *A Whole New Mind: Why Right-Brainers Will Rule the Future.* New York: Riverhead Books, 2006.

Secarcy, Tom and Henry Devries. *How to Close a Deal Like Warren Buffett: Lessons from the World's Greatest Dealmaker.* New York: McGraw-Hill, 2013.

Song, Michael, Vicki Halsey and Tim Burress. *The Hamster Revolution: How to Manage Your Email Before It Manages You.* San Francisco: Berrett-Koehler Publishers, 2008.

Williams, Greg, with Pat Iyer. *Body Language Secrets to Win More Negotiations: How to Read Any Opponent and Get What You Want.* Newburyport, MA: Career Press, 2016.

Young, James Webb. *A Technique for Producing Ideas: The Simple Five-Step Formula Anyone Can Use to Be More Creative in Business and Life.* West Valley City, UT: Waking Lion Press, 2009.

Ziesenis, Beth. *The Big Book of Apps: Your Nerdy BFF's Guide to (Almost) Every App in the Universe.* San Diego: Your Nerdy Best Friend Ink, 2017.

HEALTHCARE

Baker, Susan Keane. *Split-Second Kindness: Making a Difference When Time Is Limited.* Susan Keane Baker, 2014.

Carnarius, Megan. *A Deeper Perspective on Alzheimer's and Other Dementias: Practical Tools with Spiritual Insight.* Forres, UK: Findhorn Press, 2015.

Engel, Marcus. *The Other End of the Stethoscope: 33 Insights for Excellent Patient Care.* 3rd ed. Orlando, FL: Phillips Press, 2010.

Gittell, Jody Hoffer. *High Performance Healthcare: Using the Power of Relationships to Achieve Quality, Efficiency and Resilience.* New York: McGraw-Hill, 2009.

Hay, Louise L. *Heal Your Body: The Mental Causes for Physical Illness and the Metaphysical Way to Overcome Them.* Carlsbad, CA: Hay House, 1987.

Jonas, Wayne B., ed. *Mosby's Dictionary of Complementary and Alternative Medicine.* St. Louis, MO: Elsevier Mosby, 2005.

Malkin, Jain. *A Visual Reference for Evidence-Based Design.* Concord, CA: The Center for Health Design, 2008.

McDaniel, Derrick Y. *Eldercare: The Essential Guide to Caring for Your Loved One and Yourself.* Derrick Y. McDaniel, 2014.

Scanlan, Larry. *Hospital Mergers: Why They Work, Why They Don't Work.* Chicago: AHA Press, 2010.

PEOPLE

Brayer, Ruth. *Handwriting: Let the Power of Your Pen Change Your Life.* Ruth Brayer, 2016.

Brown, Bene. *Rising Strong: How the Ability to Reset Transforms the Way We Live, Love, Parent, and Lead.* New York: Random House, 2017.

Dillard-Wright, David. *A Mindful Day: 365 Ways to Live Life with Peace, Clarity, and an Open Heart.* Avon, MA: Adams Media, 2017.

James, Neen. *Secrets of Super-Productivity: How to Achieve Amazing Things in Your Work Life*. Doylestown, PA: Neen James Communications, 2006.

Jones, Phil M. *Exactly What to Say: The Magic Words for Influence and Impact*. Atlanta: ListenUp Audiobooks, 2017. Audible audiobook.

Keogh, Pamela, *What Would Audrey Do? Timeless Lessons for Living with Grace and Style*. London: Aurum Press, 2008.

Marshall, Margaret. *Body, Mind, Mouth: Life's Eating Connection*. Bloomington, IN: Abbott Press, 2012.

Marshall, Margaret. *Healthy Living Means Living Healthy: Lose Weight, Feel Great*. Melbourne, FL: Motivational Press, 2016.

Nelson, Marilyn Carlson. *How We Lead Matters: Reflections on a Life of Leadership*. New York: McGraw-Hill Education, 2008.

The Oprah Magazine. *Words That Matter: A Little Book of Life Lessons*. New York: HarperCollins, 2010. Kindle.

Petersen, Ralph, *Adventures of Diet Land: How to Win at the Game of Dieting from a Former Fat Guy*. Ralph Petersen, 2017.

Rosenberg, Marshall B. *Nonviolent Communication: A Language of Life*. 2nd ed. Encinitas, CA: Puddledancer Press, 2003.

Rosensweig, Jeffrey and Betty Liu. *Age Smart: Discovering the Fountain of Youth at Midlife and Beyond*. Upper Saddle River, NJ: Prentice Hall, 2006.

Scott, Howard. *Bee Lessons*. Chapel Hill, NC: Professional Press, 2002.

Zak, Paul J. *The Moral Molecule: The Source of Love and Prosperity*. New York: Penguin Group, 2012.

INDEX

connecting with stakeholders in, 129–130

construction managers and, 137–138

detailed design drafts in, 141

encouraging team creativity, 133–134

good design in, 130–133

project management software for, 139–141

schedules in, 138–139, 295

shortcomings, 128–129

projects going awry, 203–234. *See also* Healthy Project; Healthy Team

about, 203–204

budgets and, 206–207

communication breakdowns and, 211–215

due to situations out of your control, 219–226

getting back on track, 232–233

lack of team participation and, 207–210

maintaining calm when, 231–232

micromanagement and, 216–219

project controls and, 230–231, 298

scheduling and, 204–206

takeaways, 234

unforeseen developments, 226–230

protocols and responsibilities, 143–144

punch lists, 160

ABOUT THE AUTHOR

Cathy Dolan-Schweitzer is the founder and president of Health Well Done, a consulting and training company, and a recognized authority in the field of healthcare project management. She holds a master's degree in integrated medicine, with a specialty in experiential health and healing, as well as certificates in healthcare construction and emergency room design. She has also worked as special education teacher.

Cathy speaks and writes extensively about healthcare and believes that its future lies at the nexus between integrated medicine and "green" healthcare principles. Her passion is building highly functional patient-centered environments that feature elements of the natural world and offer stress-reducing sensory experiences. A resourceful, motivational, and empathetic leader, Cathy maintains a high respect for her team members and values the wisdom and experience that they bring to a project.

Throughout her 24-year career, Cathy has helped healthcare systems, providers, and other medical professionals transform the quality of their patient care through thoughtful and creative patient-centered solutions. During her time as a senior project manager at Connecticut's Stamford Hospital, she shepherded the institution through its 10-year master plan, while helping to create the physical environment that allowed it to evolve into a Planetree-designated hospital.

Underlying Cathy's *Health Well Done* project management system of *Healthy Patient, Healthy Team,* and *Healthy Project* is the recognition that the health of humanity is inextricably tied to the health of the planet, and that we must collectively respect the earth's resources while building facilities that reinforce health and wellness. She believes that this is the best way to take care of ourselves and our teams.

Cathy lives in Yonkers, New York, with her husband, Ken, her dog, Cali, and her cat, Lola. She has two beautiful, smart, confident step-daughters, Julia and Alexa, and a wonderful son-in-law, David. She loves to ski, hike, practice yoga, and motorcycle through the countryside with Ken on their Harley.

CPSIA information can be obtained
at www.ICGtesting.com
Printed in the USA
FSHW012322250519
58377FS

9 780999 250907